ALFA ROMEO
COUPÉS & SPIDERS
In Detail

ALFA ROMEO
COUPÉS & SPIDERS
In Detail
SINCE 1945

BY CHRIS REES

Herridge & Sons

Acknowledgments

Many thanks are due to my publishers, Ed and Charles Herridge, for their encouragement and forebearance, as well as for sending me boxes full of wonderful old images of Alfa Romeos. A huge debt of gratitude is owed to Michael Ward and Claire Prior at *Auto Italia* magazine for their support, plus the great number of images kindly supplied from the *Auto Italia* archive for this book. Many thanks also to Museo Storico Alfa Romeo, Fiat Chrysler Automobiles, Carrozzeria Touring, Carrozzeria Zagato, RM Sotheby's, Bonhams and Artcurial.

Published in 2019 by Herridge & Sons Ltd
Lower Forda, Shebbear
Beaworthy, Devon EX21 5SY

© Copyright Chris Rees 2019
Designed by Ray Leaning, MUSE Fine Art & Design

ISBN 978-1-906133-86-3
Printed in China

Contents

INTRODUCTION

Nicola Romeo was the financier who saved the fledgling ALFA company and added his surname to the brand's identity in 1918.

Why is it that Alfa Romeo inspires such enthusiasm among "car people"? Everyone from Henry Ford ("When I see an Alfa Romeo go by, I tip my hat") to Jeremy Clarkson ("You can't be a true petrolhead until you've owned an Alfa Romeo") understands the aura that surrounds Alfa.

So what is the intangible magic of Alfa Romeo? It's down to many things, of course. Grand Prix successes (Alfa Romeo won the first two inaugural Formula One Grand Prix championships in 1950 and 1951); advanced engineering (pioneering twin-cam technology, twin spark plugs, fuel injection and providing family cars with all-wheel disc brakes, to name a few); an unerring and innate espousal of design and aesthetics, from humble saloons to exotic race-bred supercars.

But of Alfa Romeo's many brilliant creations, it is the sports cars, above all, that have always fired the public imagination: both fixed-roof coupés and convertible spiders. In successive dynasties of coupés and spiders, Alfa Romeo has built one of the greatest canons of work of any car maker in the world. Its sports cars truly encapsulate what is great about the Italian company.

Not to decry four-door saloons – and there have been many Alfa Romeo greats in that class – it is a fact that two-door sports cars allow you to be more adventurous in design terms, and also to deliver a greater emotional impact. Italian design in general has a long history of pre-eminence, from ancient Rome onwards, and it's undeniable that Italy has produced more than its fair share of beauty in the car world, too. In the first few decades after World War Two, when Italy's design talent was arguably at its zenith, Alfa Romeo received a full complement of this creative impetus, not only from its own in-house design teams but by drawing on Italian coachbuilders like Pinin Farina, Bertone and Touring.

To say that the appeal of Alfa Romeo's sports cars lay in mere styling would be criminal, however. It was

never design alone that instilled enthusiasm in buyers; they were also drivers, and Alfa Romeo fully delivered for them, too. The Milanese company consistently displayed dizzying heights in technical terms, in many ways being in a class of its own. Time after time, Alfa Romeo plucked apparently exotic elements from very much more expensive machinery and democratised them in its own cars. Gearboxes with more ratios, cleverly selected to enhance acceleration; disc brakes on all four wheels to strengthen stopping power; lightweight aluminium engines to reduce weight; racing-style transaxles to balance that weight – the list of Alfa's pioneering innovations when other manufacturers cleaved rigidly to old conventions is extraordinary.

And all this from a manufacturer that, since the 1950s, has resolutely positioned itself, if not in the mass market, then at the popular end of what we would today call the "premium" market. Alfas have always had class; but they have also, equally importantly, been accessible to ordinary buyers.

To many people, Alfa Romeo simply means sports cars. Ask a member of the public to conjure up an image of an Alfa Romeo and they'll almost certainly think of a red Spider, top-down, driving through the countryside. Quite possibly it would be Dustin Hoffman in a Spider in *The Graduate*, or perhaps Michael Caine in an Alfa Romeo Montreal in *The Marseille Contract*. Even more likely, they'll picture themselves driving a red Alfa sports car across an evocative landscape.

This book is a celebration of Alfa's most iconic sporting machinery. There is a very good reason why it concentrates on Alfa's post-war era, for this was without doubt the most productive period for the company's coupés and sports cars; and also the era when production numbers brought Alfas to a broad cross-section of the buying public. The glory years for Alfa's sports cars were undoubtedly from the mid-1950s until the end of

the rear-wheel drive in 1994 – not forgetting, of course, that Alfa has "rediscovered" rear-wheel drive in the modern era.

We cannot ignore the fact, however, that Alfa's history of sports cars stretches right back to the birth of the company. Alfa Romeo can trace its origins back to 1910 and the creation of Anonima Lombarda Fabbrica Automobili (ALFA) – an acronym that carried no more romance than "Lombardy Automobile Manufacturing Company". The factory was in Portello, on the outskirts of Milan, on a site that would remain in use right up to 1986.

ALFA's very first car, the 24HP, was an imposing 4.1-litre four-cylinder open tourer designed by a precociously talented engineer called Giuseppe Merosi. The 24HP spawned ALFA's very first racing car, the Corsa, in 1911, while the two-seater spider model is rightly considered to be ALFA's first ever sports car.

It would be in 1913 that ALFA launched its first six-cylinder car, the 40-60HP. This then gave rise to ALFA's first Grand Prix racer in 1914, whose engine

had a specification so advanced that Alfa enthusiasts of today would recognise it, including twin camshafts and inclined valves in hemispherical combustion chambers.

ALFA had produced around 1200 cars by the outbreak of World War One, but unfortunately its financial situation was by this time pretty precarious. It is at this

Alfa Romeo's badge – seen here on a 6C 1500 SS – consists of the flag of Milan and the biscione (snake) symbol of the city's ruling Visconti family.

The engineer Giuseppe Merosi was the genius behind all early Alfas, from the 24HP onwards.

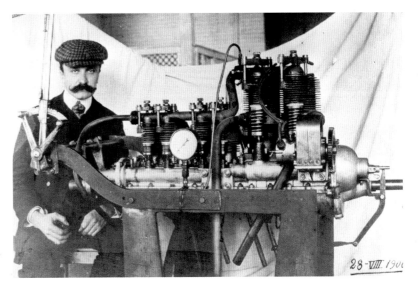

ALFA's very first model was the 24HP, which could be had in sporting body styles. This is a "Torpedo".

The 40-60HP was Alfa Romeo's first six-cylinder car. Here Giuseppe Campari competes in the 1922 Targa Florio.

point that Romeo rode in to save the day: the financier, Nicola Romeo invested money in ALFA in 1915 in order to expand production in the war effort. Signor Romeo bought the company outright in 1918, and set about turning stored-away components for approximately 100 of the old 20-30HP models into fully-built cars. These would be the very first cars to be badged "Alfa Romeo".

In 1922 Merosi conceived a new model called the RL with a 3.0-litre six-cylinder engine, a car that proved very popular in its home market. A sporty version of the RL followed, called the Super Sport (SS) and there was also a racing version called the Targa Florio (TF). The latter's victory in the 1923 Targa Florio race, with Ugo Sivocci at the wheel, was historic in more than one way. The green four-leaf clover emblems that had been applied to the car

The RL Super Sport was a lightweight, powerful sports car.

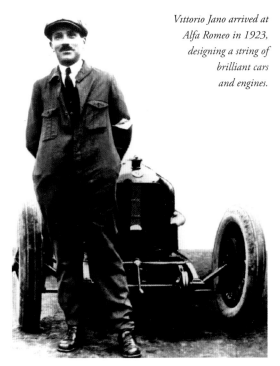

Vittorio Jano arrived at Alfa Romeo in 1923, designing a string of brilliant cars and engines.

as a good luck charm were regarded as having delivered that luck – and so they were adopted on subsequent Alfa Romeo racing cars, indelibly cementing the emblem into Alfa Romeo lore.

Duly emboldened, Alfa Romeo resumed its campaigns in Grand Prix racing. Merosi's first effort, the P1, looked promising with its twin-cam 2.0-litre six-cylinder engine – notable for its use of two spark plugs per cylinder – but a fatal crash involving Sivocci on the eve of the 1923 Italian Grand Prix ended this car's career. Merosi left the company and Nicola Romeo hired a new chief engineer in 1923 in the form of Vittorio Jano, a man who would loom large in Italy's rise to motorsport glory, not only at Alfa Romeo (where he remained until 1937) but also at Lancia and Ferrari. He was, quite simply, one of the very best engineers who ever worked with cars.

Jano's brilliance was clear in his first design for Alfa Romeo, the P2 racing car. Compact, light and aerodynamic, it was also the first Alfa to receive an eight-cylinder engine, and a supercharged one at that. The P2 won its first ever race in 1924 and bagged Alfa its first ever World Championship the following year.

Racing victories are all very well but Alfa desperately needed a road car to sell on the back of this success. Jano cleverly turned the P2's engine into a usable road unit by lopping off two of its eight cylinders and removing the supercharger. The resulting six-cylinder (6C) 1.5-litre powerplant was fitted into the new 6C 1500 road car in 1925, although it took a couple of years for it to reach production.

In 1928 came the 6C 1500 Sport model, the first Alfa Romeo road car with twin overhead camshafts, and arguably the first true Alfa sports car. This was quickly followed by the Super Sport, which boasted a shorter wheelbase and the option of a supercharger, in which case it could deliver 76hp and reach a top speed of almost 90mph.

The 6C engine expanded to 1752cc in 1929, resulting in the legendary "1750" moniker that would resonate through into Alfa's cars of the 1960s and 1970s. In its most potent supercharged Gran Sport guise, it had 85hp, and was also developed into the closed-roof Gran Turismo, an early pioneer of Alfa's sporting coupé line.

It was inevitable that Jano would return to the eight-cylinder format, which he did in 1931 by designing the 8C 2300. This straight-eight had the same internal dimensions as the 6C but an extra two cylinders and

Jano's first car for Alfa Romeo was the P2 of 1924 – a Grand Prix winner from the outset.

In Super Sport guise, the 6C 1500 was capable of almost 90mph – hugely impressive for 1928.

The 6C 1500 Sport of 1928 was a road-going sports model using a six-cylinder version of the P2 engine.

Alfa's seminal 6C 1750, seen here in supercharged Gran Sport guise.

The 8C represented Alfa's pinnacle in the 1930s. This is an 8C 2900B in full flight in the Mille Miglia race.

a supercharger. It was exceptionally powerful (up to 165hp) and high-performing (capable of up to 134mph in its ultimate Corsa specification). Its chassis, in short-wheelbase form, was ideal for coachbuilders like Zagato to create some outstandingly pretty bodywork, too. The 8C would reach its zenith in 2900 form, in the 2900A racer of 1935 and the 2900B road car of 1937. Twin superchargers and a 2905cc capacity raised power to 180hp (220hp in race tune) and formed the basis of one of the most prestigious cars of the pre-war era.

However, the 8C confirmed Alfa's drift into the upper echelons of the market – an area that was being severely squeezed during the years following the great depression. Only tiny handfuls of 8Cs were sold. Instead it would be developments of the 6C, such as the 1900 of 1933 and 2300 of 1934 – which cost less than half the price of an 8C – that would provide Alfa Romeo with its mainstay models of the 1930s.

The sometimes shaky finances of the company were stabilised by Benito Mussolini's government, which effectively bought a controlling stake in Alfa Romeo in 1933. The role of the company changed as a result. It would now be called upon to represent national pride in Grand Prix racing – not entirely successfully, it must be said – as well as taking a role in arming the nation in the build-up to war.

World War Two would prove catastrophic for Alfa Romeo, whose factories were comprehensively obliterated during bombing raids. When production restarted in the early post-war years, it was on a very

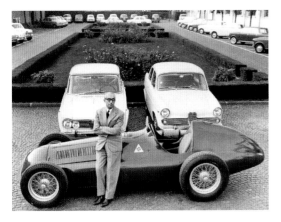

Orazio Satta Puliga joined Alfa Romeo in 1938. He was involved with the Alfetta racer and many highly significant Alfa road cars.

cars that conquered all in 1950 and 1951, but a whole string of cars that were absolutely crucial to Alfa Romeo, starting with the 1900 of 1951. Not only was this the first Alfa with an integral body/chassis, it also marked a move away from expensive, low-volume cars and towards the mass market. Alfa Romeo would offer coupé and convertible versions of the 1900: the 2+2 coupé was called Sprint, the design for which was awarded to Carrozzeria Touring; the larger Cabriolet and coupé models were officially Pinin Farina's remit.

Times moved on rapidly in the 1950s. This was the era of dream cars, and exotic creations like Touring's "Disco Volante" and Bertone's "Berlinetta Aerodinamica Tecnica" (BAT) cars fired the public imagination. But it would be a more prosaic car launched in 1954 that marked perhaps Alfa Romeo's most crucial turning point. This was not only the arrival of a truly popular

A study in aerodynamic grace: the 1938 Alfa Romeo 8C 2900B Le Mans.

The early 1950s was still an exotic era for Alfa sports cars; this is the Sportiva prototype and 1900 Super Sprint.

small scale and relied on its ageing but still seminal 6C model. This period also marked a move away from expensive coachbuilt bodywork towards a more standardised 'factory' line-up. Initially Alfa Romeo awarded contracts for its post-war coachbuilt 6Cs to Touring (coupé) and Pinin Farina (convertible). Then in 1947, the first new post-war Alfa Romeo arrived: the 6C 2500 Freccia d'Oro coupé. Unlike its coachbuilt predecessors, this model would be produced in-house at Alfa's Portello factory. Of course, independent coachbuilders continued to produce bodies on Alfa chassis, but the writing was already on the wall.

A new figure now emerged to take the company in a new direction. Orazio Satta Puliga had joined Alfa Romeo in 1938, working under Wifredo Ricart, whom he succeeded as head of design in 1946. Satta would not only mastermind the 158 and 159 Alfetta Grand Prix

A new dawn: Bertone's sensational Giulietta Sprint of 1954.

them. In car terms, spider is a lightweight, sporting roadster; the very essence of what constitutes a sports car. The Bertone-designed open-topped two-seater Giulietta Spider of 1955 was cleanly styled, fun to drive and relatively affordable.

The Spider format cemented itself as an Alfa Romeo speciality for the next five decades. For its follow-up – the Tipo 105 Giulia-based Spider of 1966 – Alfa Romeo turned to Pininfarina, rather than Bertone, and it created one of the most iconic sports car shapes of all time. Strangely, considering its considerable appeal among enthusiasts today, the design of the so-called Duetto was regarded with scepticism at launch – "a contrived design with meaningless styling gimmicks" said *Road & Track* magazine in 1966.

The Tipo 105 platform also yielded probably the most significant Alfa coupé of all time. Bertone's exquisite Sprint GT of 1963 seared itself into the consciousness of car enthusiasts with its exceptional beauty and its rewarding driveability. The 105 platform went on to form the basis of some highly successful racing cars (such as the TZ and GTA series), a four-seat convertible (the GTC) and Europe's first ever neo-classic (the Zagato Gran Sport 4R), as well as the V8-engined Montreal. Although the Bertone 105 coupé range lasted only until 1976, its place in Alfa lore is both eminent and absolutely assured in the longer term.

Alfa model – the Giulietta – but also the birth of Alfa Romeo's Spider dynasty. Why "Spider"? The word dates from the age of horse-drawn carriages, denoting a light high-wheeled trap, coined because the wheels were so large compared to the small body suspended between

The Giulia 105 spawned some exceptional sports cars. Here are Autodelta's TZ1, GTA and GTA Junior.

By the mid-1970s, it was a new-generation platform – the Alfetta Tipo 116 – that represented Alfa's fresh direction. The Alfetta was still a rear-wheel drive car but mounting the gearbox and clutch in unit with the rear axle – the so-called transaxle arrangement – was an unconventional move, harking back to Alfa's Alfetta 158/159 layout of the late 1940s and early 1950s. It provided an innately excellent weight distribution and handling balance that lent itself well to sporting applications, something that Alfa exploited with its Alfetta GT and GTV range. Arguably the Giuseppe Busso-designed V6-powered GTV 6 of 1980 was one of Alfa's all-time coupé greats, even if it was a flawed diamond.

Alfa Romeo had initially planned to end Spider production at the same time as the Giulia GT coupé range, intending it to be replaced with a new Alfetta-based sports convertible. However, that never materialised and the classic Spider simply soldiered on. Through several evolutions that centred mostly around styling and engine updates, the Spider succeeded in outlasting all its contemporaries and rivals, with a production run that spanned 1966 to 1993; in all that time, the basic underpinnings remained essentially unaltered.

Meanwhile, Alfa's "transaxle" platform also lasted longer than might have been expected. Long after the Alfetta was retired, Alfa's 75 saloon retained the signature transaxle layout. The 75 duly formed the basis of one of

Alfa's most unusual and exotic sports cars of all time, the ES 30 of 1989. This grew into the SZ, which would be Alfa's last rear-wheel drive car of the 20th century. In another revolution, albeit something of a blind alley, this was bodied in Modar, a type of plastic unique to the SZ and its soft-top development, the RZ.

The SZ marked the end of the rear-drive era, as Alfa Romeo switched to front-wheel drive. The seeds of Alfa's move to FWD had been planted back as far back as 1971 and the launch of the Alfasud. So successful a design was the Alfasud that it quickly became clear that all future compact Alfas would be front-driven, all the way from the 33 to the 145, the 156 and ultimately the MiTo and Giulietta of the 21st century. And when Alfa Romeo came to replace its long-running Spider in 1994, that would also be a front-wheel drive model, ending a line of rear-drive sporting Alfas that had continued unbroken for more than 80 years.

The new Spider would not, in fact, be based on an Alfa Romeo platform but a Fiat one. That was because, by this stage, Alfa Romeo had a new master, Fiat, to which the Italian state had finally sold the company in 1986. Alfa's engineers were directed to use the platform of the then-new Fiat Tipo as a basis for the new Tipo 916 Spider, as well as its sister coupé model, the GTV. This radical-looking Pininfarina-designed pairing was as modern as the classic Spider had been old-fashioned, and

Spider generations: from 1966 Duetto to 2010 Spider.

The last rear-wheel drive Spider Series 4 contrasts with its front-wheel drive successors, the 916 and Brera-based Spider.

drove very differently, too. The Tipo 916 also marked a move back to V6 power, the classic Alfa Busso V6 now powering the front wheels for the first time.

But the front-drive era would prove to be short-lived. The Alfa 156-based GT of 2003 was in fact the last new exclusively front-drive coupé that Alfa conceived. In 2005 came another historic debutant: the 159-based Brera, historic because it was offered with four-wheel drive. Although this was certainly not the first-ever Alfa built with 4x4, it was the first sports car with all wheels driven, something that the new Spider of 2006 also repli-cated. Alfa's history of linking up with other companies continued, because by this point the Fiat Group was co-operating closely with General Motors, and GM

Alfa Romeo drew parallels between its SZ of 1989 and the pre-war 1750.

supplied much of Alfa's engine technology, while the 4x4 platform had originally been conceived to underpin a new Saab.

Then it was back to rear-wheel drive in 2008, with the launch of the 8C Competizione. Once again, there was another new relationship, this time with Maserati. The famous Italian prestige car maker had been bought by Fiat in 1993, which then passed it on to Ferrari (also owned by Fiat). In yet another merry-go-round move, Maserati was split away from Ferrari in 2005 to be partnered up with Alfa Romeo to form the so-called "Maserati and Alfa Romeo Group". Maserati's 4200 coupé duly provided the basis for the low-volume Alfa 8C Competizione coupé and Spider models.

When production of the GT, Brera and Brera-based Spider ended in 2010, Alfa Romeo was left without either a coupé or an open-topped model in its range for pretty much the only time in its entire 100-year history (other than a few brief months in 1994, that is). That startling state affairs was soon addressed, however, for yet another revolutionary model arrived in 2013 when Alfa Romeo announced the 4C. This was a mid-engined sports car – only Alfa's second centrally-engined model after the 33 Stradale. Firsts also stacked up in terms of

its construction (it was a carbon-fibre monocoque) and body style (the 4C Spider launched in 2014 was Alfa's first ever targa roof model).

At the time of writing, the 4C Spider is the only sports car in Alfa Romeo's range. However, the company has signalled it has no intention of leaving this market segment. In a five-year plan set out by CEO Sergio Marchionne in 2018, two new coupé models were due to be launched by 2022: the mid-engined 8C (with the option of 700hp hybrid power and four-wheel drive) and the GTV (effectively a two-door coupé version of the Giulia saloon).

So here is the story of Alfa Romeo's two-door cars in the post-war era. It's a story of engineering endeavour, aesthetic intelligence, commercial bravery and a willingness to experiment. But to answer the question at the beginning of my introduction – "What is the intangible magic of Alfa Romeo?" – it's about passion. From the people who conceived, designed and brought to market these exceptional cars to the people who purchased them in period, and the enthusiasts who continue to appreciate and enjoy them today, passion is the one thread that joins it all together. Passion: this is the ineffable and elusive quality that truly defines Alfa Romeo.

The 4C Spider is Alfa's last remaining sports car in production (at the time of writing), seen next to the 1967 33 Stradale.

Chapter One

6C:
SPORTING SPIRIT

This book begins, not with a glorious dawn, but with the dying embers of a bygone era for Alfa Romeo. World War 2 had seen the company's factories turned over mostly to the war effort. Even though its Portello plant was heavily bombed in a series of raids in 1943-1944, production did manage to stumble on spasmodically. Most of the vehicles made during the war were Coloniale military staff cars but some examples of Alfa's 6C 2500 were also made (47 units in 1943, 18 in 1944 and five in 1945). It's thought that some 339 Alfa Romeos were produced from 1941 to 1945.

When hostilities ceased, all sinews were bent

L'Alfa Romeo 6 c - 2300 B Mille Miglia 4 posti è la vettura di serie più veloce che vi permetterà i più rapidi spostamenti nei vostri viaggi di gran turismo

Direzione e Officine: Via M. U. Traiano, 33 · Milano

An advert for the 6C 2300B coupé Mille Miglia.

towards restarting car production, and it took Alfa remarkably little time to get its lines working again. Unsurprisingly, the 6C 2500 that Alfa began offering in 1945 was very little different from the pre-war version. The 6C 2500 was the ultimate expression of Alfa Romeo's long and highly successful dynasty of six-cylinder models. While the eight-cylinder model line, typified by the 8C 2300, marked the company's confidently upmarket zenith, Alfa realised that it had to pursue a more pragmatic path in these tougher post-war times and so favoured the 6C over the 8C.

Developed under the supervision of Bruno

Evocative publicity for the 6C 2300B Mille Miglia proclaims it to be the "arrow" of the Mille Miglia race.

The 6C 2300 effectively replaced the eight-cylinder 8C 2300.

The elegant proportions of the 1938 6C 2300B coupé were clear.

Trevisan, the 6C 2500 had been launched in 1939 as the very last of the six-cylinder Alfa line conceived by Vittorio Jano. He had started with a 1487cc straight-six double overhead camshaft engine in Alfa's 6C 1500 of 1927, expanding that to 1752cc for the legendary 6C 1750 of 1929, then to 1917cc for the 6C 2000 of 1933, and then to 2309cc in 1934 for the 6C 2300 model (which effectively replaced the eight-cylinder 8C 2300).

In its ultimate 6C 2500 guise, launched in 1939, the engine reached a capacity of 2443cc thanks to an enlarged bore of 72m and an unchanged stroke of 100mm, and could develop 87hp. Its under-square dimensions delivered beefy low-down torque, while the four-speed column-change gearbox had four ratios, third and fourth being synchronised.

In terms of construction, this model followed the general layout of earlier Alfas: a strong box-section

frame, parallel front trailing arms with coil springs, and rear swing axles with longitudinal torsion bars. The chassis was offered in three distinct wheelbase lengths. The Turismo was 3250mm long and was

The 6C Freccia d'Oro ("Golden Arrow") of 1947 was Alfa's first post-war design.

17

The Freccia d'Oro lived up to its name; a study in restrained elegance.

It was designed as a grand tourer rather than an out-and-out sports car, and could seat six.

The 6C 2500 GT brochure proclaims the model's triple-carburettor engine.

In 1950, the 6C 2500 was upgraded to become the Gran Turismo, with a new notchback body style.

Carrozzeria Touring created the sportiest 6C 2500 Super Sport model of all, the Villa d'Este.

With its 2.5-litre 105hp Super Sport engine, the Villa d'Este was a genuine 100mph car.

offered with saloon or limousine bodywork.

The Sport version, meanwhile, had its wheelbase cut to 3000mm and proved perfect for a variety of coachbuilt bodywork, from saloons to coupés to convertibles. The attractions for coachbuilders were made all the more powerful by the Sport's single-carburettor engine developing a healthier 95hp – although poor fuel quality in the post-war period forced Alfa to reduce the compression ratio, so power fell to 90hp. Despite being a very large and rather heavy machine (typically around 1.5 tonnes), it was capable of a top speed of 95mph. Some 779 Sport models were made between 1939 and 1952, most of them in two-seater coupé and convertible forms by independent coachbuilders.

The most focused model in the range was the Super Sport, initially born as a racing version with a wheelbase shortened to 2700mm. The 1939 Corsa racing car had an engine tuned up to 125hp at 4800rpm, while a coupé version raced at Le Mans in 1939 and both spiders and coupés ran in the 1940 Mille Miglia.

In road-going form, the Super Sport's engine featured three carburettors and a power output of 110hp, although as with the Sport version, fuel quality issues after the war meant Alfa reduced the compression ratio from 8:1 to 7.5:1 and power dropped to 105hp from 1947. Nonetheless, this was a car that could comfortably exceed 100mph.

Available as a chassis for coachbuilders from 1939, the Super Sport was included on Alfa Romeo's price list officially from 1946 as its range-topper. Alfa offered a Touring-bodied coupé as a model in its own range from this time, which underwent a series of improvements in the following years, culminating in its being called Villa d'Este in 1949.

Meanwhile, the official contract for a convertible version went to Pinin Farina, which adapted its coachbuilt Sport chassis design for the Super Sport. Farina went on to make over 150 units of this style. Some 458 examples of the 6C Super Sport were made up until 1952.

It would not be until 1947 that the first new post-war Alfa Romeo arrived – and it was a coupé. Using the 6C 2500 Sport chassis (3000mm wheelbase), Alfa's Portello works produced the 6C 2500 Freccia d'Oro ("Golden Arrow"). This was an imposing five-seat coupé with fastback bodywork in pressed steel. It boasted an extremely comfortable and luxurious interior that was also rather spacious for a car with grand touring pretensions; it could easily take three passengers up front and a further three in the back (albeit with a bit of a squeeze).

The all-independent suspension provided predictable handling but the steering was often criticised for being lifeless and heavy. There was plenty of body roll in corners but the clever geometry of the swing axles

Touring's streamlined, lightweight Villa d'Este shape was preferred by sporting drivers.

Here is a 6C 2500 Super Sport bodied by Touring in 1948.

meant that corners could be negotiated with confidence. As ever, the column gearchange was one of the less attractive features of the 6C, but the hydraulically-operated drum brakes worked solidly well.

In 1950, the Freccia d'Oro – of which 680 examples were made in all, many of them delivered to movie stars and royalty – evolved into the Gran Turismo with various styling changes, notably transforming it into a three-box coupé rather than a fastback. At the same time, the 105hp Super Sport engine was adopted as standard, making it a genuine 100mph car.

The 6C 2500 range remained in production until 1953, some two years after its replacement, the 1900, had been launched.

SPECIFICATIONS

6C 2500
FRECCIA D'ORO/GRAN TURISMO

Engine:	2443cc 6-cyl in-line twin-cam
Power:	90-93hp @ 4600rpm
	105hp @ 4800rpm
Torque:	N/A
Transmission:	4-speed manual
Wheels:	18in steel (17in from 1949)
Weight:	1075kg (chassis only)
Max speed:	96mph/100mph
0-62mph	N/A

Coachbuilt models

The low floorline of the 2500 gave it particular appeal for independent coachbuilders. A huge variety of carrozzerie adopted the 6C 2500 chassis, including Pinin Farina, Ghia, Castagna, Boneschi and, perhaps most notably, Carrozzeria Touring. The latter's Superleggera construction method of light metal tubes allowed for some of the most sporting variants on the 6C 2500 Super Sport chassis, perhaps the ultimate being the Villa d'Este model of 1949, whose pillarless side windows were a major advance at the time. Touring also offered an "Aerlux" version with a transparent roof hinged at its trailing edge that could be tilted open a few inches.

In profile, the proportional superiority of Touring's Villa d'Este coupé is plain to see.

Touring also made this convertible version of its Villa d'Este.

Stabilimenti Farina was one of several coachbuilders to clothe the 6C 2500 chassis in its own distinctive style.

Chapter Two

1900:

ALFA'S POPULIST CONTENDER

In the immediate post-war years, Alfa Romeo continued to pursue the same pre-war path of motorsport-inspired glory and hand-built road cars for wealthy clients that had worked so well for it before the war. But the management quickly realised that Europe in post-war times was a very different place, with very different needs. In 1950 it committed itself to a future based on bringing motoring to the masses – or the slightly less well-heeled, at any rate – with a highly significant new model: the 1900.

Importantly, the 1900 was the first Alfa to have integral body/chassis construction, rather than a separate chassis, giving it all sorts of advantages in terms of weight, stiffness, ease of construction and performance. The 1900 four-door saloon was conceived by Alfa's Chief Engineer, Orazio Satta

The 1900 Berlina marked a complete revolution for Alfa Romeo, in terms of its unitary construction and its target audience.

Puliga, and had engineering prowess writ large upon it, if not necessarily aesthetic elegance. Revealed at the 1950 Paris Motor Show, the 1900 was very well received from the outset, even if it never sold in the numbers Alfa had hoped for; some 21,304 examples of all types were made from 1950 to 1959, saloons accounting for 17,390 of that total.

One major change for Alfa was that the 1900 marked a switch from six cylinders to four. If that sounded like a move downmarket, it was; but in engineering terms it certainly wasn't. One of the people involved in the new engine was another of Alfa Romeo's legendary talents, Giuseppe Busso, who had originally joined Alfa Romeo in 1939, before leaving to join Enzo Ferrari and help to develop the Ferrari 125 V12 engine. Busso had rejoined Alfa in 1948

The Touring designed Sprint in its original (Series 1) guise of 1951.

and the 1900 engine was one of his most important projects. The iron-block, alloy-head four-cylinder engine displaced 1884cc and developed a healthy 90hp at 5200rpm.

In contrast to the relatively advanced engine, rather less impressive was the antique-feeling column-shift four-speed gearbox. However, the suspension design marked another leap forward for Alfa Romeo. The front end used wishbones and coil springs, while the rear live axle was located by trailing arms and coils – far more sophisticated than the typical leaf springs of the period.

Almost immediately, 1900 berlinas enjoyed racing success in events as diverse as the Carrera Panamericana and the Mille Miglia. Alfa's very first model badged TI (standing for Turismo Internazionale) arrived in 1951, boasting a more powerful 100hp engine with bigger valves, a higher compression ratio and a twin-choke carburettor. Loved by amateur racers, the 1900 TI was advertised as "the family car that wins races".

In 1951, Rudolf Hruska arrived at Portello, bringing with him huge experience of production practices at Porsche and other companies, which he put into operation with the 1900, at the same time reducing Alfa's costs. Hruska would have a big impact at Alfa Romeo in future years, particularly with the Giulietta and Alfasud, but those stories are for later chapters.

The 1900 was elevated to 1900 Super status in 1953, with an engine expanded to 1975cc by increasing its bore to 84.5mm. In standard guise, its 90hp output was unchanged but the Super TI version's power was boosted to 115hp at 5000rpm thanks to two twin-choke carbs.

Coachbuilders leapt on the 1900, even though it didn't have a separate chassis. As well as the stan-dard-wheelbase (or 1900L) platform, Alfa Romeo created a 1900C (C standing for Corto, or Short) chassis especially for coachbuilders, with a wheelbase measuring 2500mm (versus 2630mm in the saloon). A small number of Primavera two-door saloons (281 in total) were sold from 1955, but in contrast to most of the sportier coupés described below, this model sat on the longer wheelbase of the four-door saloon.

Three different body styles of 1900 Sprint on show, alongside the 1900 Berlina.

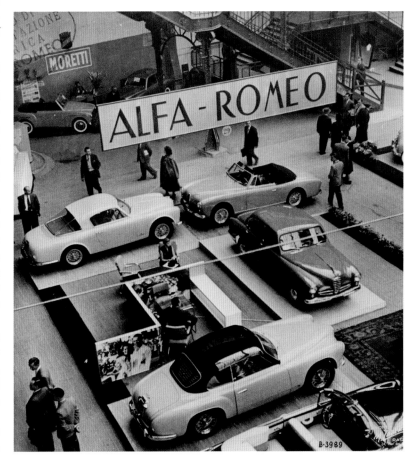

The later, much revised 1900 Super Sprint (SS) of 1955.

1900C SPRINT COUPÉ/CABRIOLET (1951-1955) & 1900C SUPER SPRINT COUPÉ/ SPIDER (1954-1958)

The general manager at Alfa Romeo, Iginio Alessio, assiduously worked in tandem with Italy's carrozzerie to make the 1900 unibody chassis work for them. From 1951, coachbuilders used the 1900 TI engine and shorter-wheelbase 1900C (Corto) chassis, with its wheelbase of 2500mm, to create sporty new coach-

work (see separate section on Coachbuilt 1900s).

But as with the old 6C 2500, Alfa Romeo wanted to offer its own sports models in an official capacity. It gave the contract to build the so-called 1900C Sprint 2+2 coupé to Carrozzeria Touring of Milan, while Pinin Farina got the nod for an elegant four-seat 1900C Cabriolet and coupé.

Touring made good use of its patented Superleggera principle of light aluminium panelling over a

Floor-mounted gearchange for the 1900C Sprint was a big advance on Alfa's previous column change.

Pinin Farina's Cabriolet of 1951 was perhaps the least aesthetically accomplished of the official Alfa 1900 models.

tubular steel frame. There were in fact four separate types of Touring-bodied 1900 coupé. Series 1 cars had longer doors than the later Series 2 version, along with flush door handles. Series 3 cars moved up to the 1975cc engine introduced in the 1900 Super in 1953, and had bigger front brakes, larger windows and different front side vents. Series 4 cars had a completely different shape, with one window per side rather than previous two-window config-uration, and more streamlined rear end treatment. In terms of production numbers, Touring bodied approximately 300, 158, 477 and 571 of each series respectively. Touring also made several unique bodies in addition to the "official" Sprint.

Meanwhile, Pinin Farina's Cabriolet and coupé, offered from 1952, were rather more austere in shape, and certainly simpler. The coupé had very thick C-pillars, alleviated somewhat by a wraparound rear window. The Cabriolet was distin-guished by a slight kink in the rear wing waistline (although Farina also did offer alternative body styles itself). Pinin Farina made a total of 88 Cabrio-lets and 100 coupés.

In 1954 came the 1900C Super Sprint (or SS), effectively replacing the earlier Sprint. This adopted the mechanicals of the 1900 TI Super Berlina, the main advances being the enlarged 1975cc engine (in

SS spec developing 112hp) and five-speed gearbox with closer-spaced ratios and a taller final drive ratio (in place of the old four-speed unit). The SS was now a formidable performer, capable of a top speed of 118mph. Only 614 examples of the Super Sprint chassis were built up until 1958.

The Pinin Farina 1900C coupé was a more formal, sober effort than Touring's.

Pinin's curved rear screen was something of a novelty for the time.

S P E C I F I C A T I O N S	
1900C	
SPRINT	
Engine:	1884cc 4-cyl twin-cam
Power:	100hp at 5500rpm
Torque:	N/A
Transmission:	4-speed manual
Wheels:	16in steel
Weight:	1050-1150kg
Max speed:	112mph
0-62mph:	N/A

S P E C I F I C A T I O N S	
1900C	
SUPER SPRINT	
Engine:	1975cc 4-cyl twin-cam
Power:	112hp at 5900rpm
Torque:	146Nm (108lb ft) @ 3600rpm
Transmission:	5-speed manual
Wheels:	16in steel
Weight:	1000-1100kg
Max speed:	118mph
0-62mph:	N/A

The stunning 1900C SS Speciale built by Boano in 1955 for Argentina's president, Juan Perón.

Audacious rear end treatment marked the 1900C SS Speciale.

COACHBUILT 1900s

Although Touring and Farina made most of the coachbuilt bodywork for the 1900C Sprint and Super Sprint chassis, there were dozens of other independent efforts. Carrozzeria Zagato made a model (unofficially called the 1900 SSZ) targeted at racing. Its lightweight aluminium body was notably aerodynamic and featured Zagato's trademark double-bubble roof. Around 40 examples of the SSZ were made in all.

A team from Ghia, including Mario Boano and Virgil Exner, created the American-influenced 1900C Gioello (jewel) coupé, some 10 of which were made from 1953. Ghia also offered the more conventional-looking Supergioiello coupé on the longer 1900L chassis, offering four seats, while Gian Paolo Boano designed a rather heavy-looking effort for Ghia in 1954. Giovanni Savonuzzi's 1900C Super Sprint coupé of 1955 was the most successful Ghia offering on the 1900 – perhaps a dozen of these were made.

Bertone's 1900C Sprint-based Perla spider of 1955 was particularly elegant, although its rear fins made it look less fetching than Bertone's Giulietta Spider presented the same year.

Other limited-production and one-off bodies abounded. Boneschi built the Astral spider in 1953, two of which were made, one being delivered to Rafael Trujillo, the dictator of the Dominican Republic. Another "dictator" car was created by Boano: the extraordinary 1900C SS coupé Sport in 1955, with a huge curved glass rear window, of which only two were made (one with a 6C 2300 engine for the Argentinian president, Juan Perón). Boano followed this one

Ghia's 1953 Sprint Gioiello was typical of the Turin coachbuilder's work.

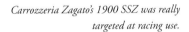

Carrozzeria Zagato's 1900 SSZ was really targeted at racing use.

The Supergioiello was a more conventional Ghia effort on the long-wheelbase 1900L chassis.

A certain US influence marked Ghia-Aigle's 1900 2+2 coupé of 1958.

Boneschi's outlandish Astral convertible.

This 1951 Cabriolet by Stabilimenti Farina was conservative in taste.

The 1955 "Perla" clearly presaged the Giulietta Spider that Bertone would present the same year.

This unusual Pinin Farina 1900 coupé remained a one-off.

Boneschi's Gazzella of 1953 was based on the 1900L platform.

Half-way between a saloon and a coupé: a Bertone 1900L-based effort from 1953.

a year later with a no less exceptional design featuring rear fins, but most of its 1900C production was rather more conventional in appearance. Both coupés and spiders were made.

Swiss company Ghia-Aigle made several one-offs, mostly designed by Giovanni Michelotti; these included convertibles and coupés, plus a roof-less barchetta. Vignale made a 1900 Spider called La Fleche, while Fantuzzi designed the outlandish Gazzella, and Worblaufen, Colli, Castagna and Francis Lombardi also tried their hands.

Many coupés and cabriolets were also offered on the standard wheelbase (or "1900L") platform. Bertone's effort of 1953 was somewhat sober, as was Boneschi's Gazzella of 1952. Pinin Farina designed an unusual 2+2 coupé on the 1900L in 1954, which curiously did without an Alfa *scudetto* (grille) or even an Alfa badge.

Aptly named the Disco Volante ("Flying Saucer") was this 1952 aerodynamic spider.

Of the five Disco Volantes built, only one had a fixed roof.

FLYING SAUCERS, BATS & SPORTIVAS

Touring was the design house behind the extraordinary 1900 C52 Disco Volante (Flying Saucer) of 1952. Conceived for racing, its bodywork, built around a specific tubular space frame, was tested in the wind tunnel to be aerodynamically efficient even in crosswinds, with an extreme degree of side body shaping and a flat under-body.

The engine had an aluminium block with inserted liners, a bore expanded to 85mm for a 1997cc capacity, a higher compression ratio and two twin-choke carburettors. That meant it was capable of 158hp, and a top speed of 220km/h (140mph) was quoted. Five Disco Volantes were built, only one of which was given a coupé roof, while two had a 3495cc double overhead cam straight-six engine from the Alfa Romeo 6C 3000 CM racing car.

Some of the most striking specials of all time were Bertone's BAT series, designed by Franco Scaglione. BAT stood for *Berlinetta Aerodinamica Tecnica*,

denoting their role as aerodynamic test concepts – with a drag coefficient as low as 0.19. The first of the three cars built – BAT 5 – was presented at the 1953 Turin Show. With its smooth front end, enclosed wheels and tapering fins, it represented cutting edge aerodynamic theory at the time, boasting a drag coefficient of 0.23. Although based on the 1900, its five-speed gearbox and slippery shape enabled a top speed of 120mph. BAT 7 arrived in 1954 with a lower

Bertone's unparalleled Berlinetta Aerodinamica Tecnica triplet of experimental cars.

Designed by Franco Scaglione, the first of the three BAT cars built – BAT 5 – was presented in 1953.

1954's BAT 7 had big tail fins and a claimed drag coefficient of just 0.19.

The final BAT 9 of 1955 looked a little less like a sci-fi film prop.

Another Franco Scaglione designed prototype: the 1900 Sport Spider of 1954.

The so-called 2000 Sportiva coupé was judged to be too expensive to produce in series.

nose and large tail fins (and reputedly a drag coefficient of just 0.19), while 1955's BAT 9 had a cleaner, more conventional shape with scaled-down fins.

Alfa Romeo also called on Bertone for its 1954 prototypes for a new coupé and spider. Franco Scaglione designed the bodywork which was realised in aluminium. The first of these was the 1900 Sport Spider, while the coupé version was dubbed 2000 Sportiva. Powered by the same 1997cc twin-cam engine as in the 1900 C52 Disco Volante, it had a power output of 138hp and a top speed of 137mph. The light all-aluminium bodywork (the car weighed a mere 910kg) was mounted atop a Disco Volante-based spaceframe chassis. This was intended as a production car and potential racer, but Alfa Romeo made only four prototypes (two spiders and two coupés). The reason? It would have been an exorbi-

tantly expensive model to produce and the company decided its attentions would be far better diverted towards the forthcoming Giulietta Sprint – almost certainly the correct call.

It was one of the great lost "might have beens".

Chapter Three

2000 TIPO 102 & 2600 TIPO 106:

LUXURY AND STYLE

After just a few years on sale, the 1900 was updated by Alfa Romeo to become the Tipo 102 2000 Berlina. This was launched at the 1957 Turin Motor Show, although production would not begin until 1958, and like the 1900, the 2000's construction was of unitary steel, although it had a much more modern appearance.

Alfa had already rejected the 1900 Sport Spider and 2000 Sportiva prototypes (see previous chapter) as production propositions, deeming them too difficult and expensive to make in series. Instead, they developed a Spider convertible version of the new 2000 Berlina. This was launched in 1958 and bore the chassis code 102.04. A Sprint coupé model (chassis code 102.05) followed the Spider, but it would not be until 1960 that it found its way on to Alfa's price lists. As with the 1900, both sporty 2000 models were based on a shorter platform than the saloon's 2720mm wheelbase, but the Spider's was now even shorter than

the Sprint's (2500mm versus 2580mm).

As Alfa's flagship, the 2000 was quite an exotic car by contemporary standards. Only 2799 Berlinas were made from 1958 to 1962, making them rarer than the 1958-1961 Spider (of which 3443 examples were made), while the 1960-1962 Sprint was the rarest of all (704 made).

At the 1962 Geneva Motor Show, the 2000 was replaced by the 2600 Tipo 106 family, launched simultaneously in three body styles: Berlina saloon, Spider convertible and Sprint coupé. All three inherited their bodywork from their corresponding 2000 predecessors, albeit with minor facelifts. Easily the most significant change was a switch from four cylinders to six. This would in fact be the very last Alfa to be made with an in-line six-cylinder engine. The 2584cc engine had all-alloy construction and was, unusually for Alfa, over-square (with a shorter stroke than bore).

The 2000 Berlina launched in 1957 was effectively a much updated version of the 1900.

New in 1960 was the six-cylinder 2600 Berlina, an expensive, exclusive saloon.

Alfa's flagship 2600 models felt pretty antiquated by the time they left production in 1968. Since the more modern Giulia-based models were selling so well, Alfa Romeo decided not to replace the 2600 range directly.

2000 SPIDER (1957-1961)

While the four-door 2000 Berlina was manufactured at the Alfa Romeo factory, the Spider was handed over to Carrozzeria Touring, in terms of both its design and body manufacture. Some 3443 examples would be made by Touring from 1957 to 1961 – a healthy number – indeed, it actually outsold the 2000 Berlina. This was particularly impressive as its 2,500,000 lire price tag was 25% higher than the contemporary Giulietta Spider's.

The well-resolved body design was by Touring's Felice Bianchi Anderloni. The 2500mm wheelbase (220mm shorter than the 2600 saloon's) helped the

Felice Bianchi Anderloni's Spider design was elegant, and its soft-top made it ideal for touring.

Carrozzeria Touring not only designed the 2000 Spider but also manufactured it.

There was perhaps a touch of Ferrari about the Alfa 2000 Spider when viewed from the rear.

proportions look supremely elegant, although there was some criticism of the slightly fussy dual chrome body lines to the sides. The 2000 Spider was always a pure two-seater with a folding soft top (or, as an option, a removable hardtop).

The 2.0-litre engine was essentially a carry-over of the later-type 1900's four-cylinder unit. This measured 1975cc in capacity and retained the basic layout of a cast iron block with an aluminium head, plus two chain-driven overhead camshafts. With its single carburettor, engine power in the saloon was 105hp at 5300rpm, but in the Spider (and indeed the later Sprint coupé), that rose to 115hp at 5700rpm courtesy of two Solex side-draught carburettors and a higher compression ratio. A creditable top speed of 110mph was possible.

The five-speed gearbox boasted synchromesh on all forward speeds. In contrast to the Berlina's column-

Alfa's 1975cc engine had four cylinders and 115hp.

A classic 1950s Italian sports car cabin: elegant and luxurious but also focused.

mounted gearshift, adopted to allow room for three people to sit abreast up front, the two-door models had the gear lever relocated to the floor.

Front suspension was independent by double wishbones, while the rear axle was live, with all four corners using coil springs and telescopic dampers. Braking was by hydraulically operated drums. While the 2000 Spider may have lacked the incisive handling of its smaller Giulietta Spider sister, and was often criticised for its heavy steering at low speeds, it was an excellent touring vehicle by the standards of the day.

Lovely 1961 advert for the 2000 Spider suggests you'll feel like a racing champion driving it.

SPECIFICATIONS

2000 SPIDER

Engine:	1975cc 4-cyl twin-cam
Power:	115hp @ 5900rpm
Torque:	146Nm (108lb ft) @ 3600rpm
Transmission:	5-speed manual
Weight:	1260kg
Max speed:	106mph
0-62mph:	11.2sec

The 2000 Sprint was the very first production car designed by Giorgetto Giugiaro.

2000 SPRINT (1960-1962)

First presented at the end of 1959 and put into production in 1960, the coupé version of the 2000 range was dubbed Sprint. This was the very first car designed by Giorgetto Giugiaro while at Bertone, and was widely regarded as a triumph of pared-back elegance and good proportions. Twin headlamps, with the inner pair smaller than the outer pair, were a successful styling innovation.

In terms of the powertrain, the Sprint shared the Spider's 115hp engine and five-speed gearbox, but its wheelbase was some 80mm longer (2580mm). This helped give the Sprint enough space inside to seat four people, making it an appealing prospect for grand touring in comfort at speed.

The 2000 Sprint was built for Alfa Romeo at the Bertone works and was a rare machine with only 704 made up until 1962. Between 1958 and 1961, Vignale also offered its own coachbuilt Alfa 2000 coupé, with styling by Giovanni Michelotti. Based on chassis stamped 102.02 (distinct from series cars), it's thought that around 15 Vignale-bodied cars were made.

Its slightly longer wheelbase than the Spider's gave the Sprint enough space to seat four.

S P E C I F I C A T I O N S	
2000 SPRINT	
Engine:	1975cc 4-cyl twin-cam
Power:	115hp @ 5900rpm
Torque:	146Nm (108lb ft) @ 3600rpm
Transmission:	5-speed manual
Weight:	1300kg
Max speed:	106mph
0-62mph:	11.5sec

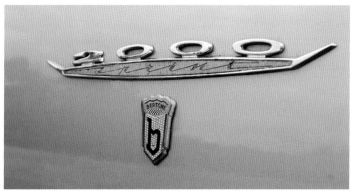

The shape was widely viewed as a masterpiece of understated coupé elegance.

The 2000 Sprint lasted in production until 1962, with only 704 examples made.

FNM ONÇA

Brazil had its own version of the Alfa Romeo 2000 Berlina from 1960 onwards, courtesy of Fábrica Nacional de Motores (FNM). However, things might have gone further in 1965 when a coupé developed entirely by FNM called the Onça was developed. Designed by Genaro Malzoni, it resembled somewhat the Ford Mustang but was based on the FNM 2000 (and thus by extension, the Alfa 2000), and had an Alfa-style grille. However, Alfa Romeo management in Italy insisted on testing the car before giving the project its blessing, but that never materialised. Only five examples of the FNM Onça were ever built.

The Brazilian "Alfa Romeo Mustang", the ultra-rare FNM Onça.

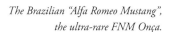

The 2600 Spider may not have looked much different to its 2000 predecessor, but it packed six-cylinder punch.

2600 SPIDER (1962-1965)

The larger-engined 2600 Spider launched in 1962 looked very much like the previous 2000 model. Its Carrozzeria Touring body had only minor changes, such as smaller front grilles, the loss of body side cooling vents, a single bonnet vent rather than two, a full-width front bumper, and the deletion of chrome body strips. The 2600 Spider did mark one significant change, in that its cabin had seating for 2+2 rather than being a strict two-seater, although it must be said the two rear seats were pretty cramped.

In the saloon, the 2584cc straight-six all-alloy engine had a single carburettor and developed 132hp, but in the Spider and Sprint, that was upped to 145hp, courtesy of three Solex twin-choke carbs and a higher 9:1 compression ratio. That meant the 2600 Spider was good for 122mph. The larger engine was heavier than the old "four", with good and bad effects: it improved straight-line stability but had a deleterious effect on handling and, in particular, low-speed steering effort. Journalist Martin Buckley commented: "While you almost 'think' an Alfa 105 coupé through corners, the determinedly understeering 2600 just

feels a heftier, less wieldy car. It's under-tyred for its weight and power and has hefty, ponderous low-speed steering… like a 1950s car."

The Spider was actually priced below the Sprint (£2745 in the UK in 1962) but even so, the coupé outsold the drop-top by three to one; some 2257 convertibles were made in all, of which around 100 were right-hand drive. Its main problem was that the contemporary Giulietta Spider (see Chapter 4) was more handsome, better handling and cheaper.

SPECIFICATIONS	
2600 SPIDER	
Engine:	2584cc V6 twin-cam
Power:	145hp @ 5900rpm
Torque:	184Nm (136lb ft) @ 2000rpm
Transmission:	5-speed manual
Weight	1330kg
Max speed:	122mph
0-62mph:	9.8sec

Slightly less fussy detailing distinguished the 2600 from the 2000.

The triple-carb, all-alloy 2584cc straight-six engine developed a healthy 145hp.

Some 6999 examples of the 2600 Sprint were built, making it the most popular 2600 variant of all.

2600 SPRINT (1962-1966)

The 2600 Sprint very much followed in the tracks of the previous 2000 Sprint, and its Bertone styling hardly changed – which was a good thing in most people's books, as it was such a great looker. Among the very minor updates were new air intakes in the bonnet and front valance. Early Sprints used front disc brakes and rear drums, but in 1965, after some 4089 cars had been built, that switched to all-round discs.

A grand total of 6999 examples of the 2600 Sprint were built in all, making it easily the most popular version in the 2600 range; some 597 were right-hand drive. A pretty prototype convertible based on the Sprint was shown by Bertone in 1963 but it didn't reach production. Some 2600 Sprints were used by the Italian police as patrol cars and many featured as such in contemporary films.

The 2600 Sprint made an ideal police pursuit vehicle.

SPECIFICATIONS	
2600 SPRINT	
Engine:	2584cc V6 twin-cam
Power:	145hp @ 5900rpm
Torque:	184Nm (136lb ft) @ 2000rpm
Transmission:	5-speed manual
Weight:	1370kg
Max speed:	118mph
0-62mph:	10.0sec

The production 2600 SZ looked far more resolved after Ercole Spada of Zagato had reworked it.

One of the prototypes of the 2600 SZ, which proved so controversial that it was ultimately redesigned.

SPECIFICATIONS	
2600 SZ	
Engine:	2584cc V6 twin-cam
Power:	145hp @ 5900rpm
Torque :	184Nm (136lb ft) @ 2000rpm
Transmission:	5-speed manual
Weight:	1250kg
Max speed:	122mph
0-62mph:	9.7sec

2600 SZ (1965-1967)

Zagato essayed its own Alfa Romeo-sanctioned version of the 2600, the Sprint Zagato or SZ. The shape was the work of Ercole Spada of Zagato. When it was first shown at the 1962 Turin Motor Show in prototype form, its extraordinary looks – to the point of being downright ugly – drew plenty of criticism. Thankfully it was refined, over quite a long gestation period, to become a much happier-looking shape for the production version, which was launched as an official Alfa Romeo model in 1965. The prototype's controversial

While it was typically aerodynamic, Zagato's SZ was not as lightweight as it would have liked it to be.

headlamp cowls were replaced by lights set back in stainless steel shrouds, the bonnet was more conventional in shape, and the original cut-off tail was made rather happier. Black-painted sills toned down the bulky look of the side profile.

The SZ was based on the short 2500mm wheelbase of the 2600 Spider. Overall, it ended up being substantially shorter, lower and narrower than the regular Sprint coupé. However, Alfa Romeo insisted that the SZ should have steel bodywork, rather than Zagato's normal choice of aluminium; as a result, while overall weight was reduced, it was only by 120kg compared to the 2600 Sprint. Since its 145hp power

output was shared with the regular 2600 and the five-speed gearbox kept the same ratios, it didn't perform quite as well as might have been expected. That was exacerbated by aerodynamics that did not permit the target top speed of 150mph. Instead, the SZ ended up maxing out at 122mph, only fractionally faster than the Sprint.

The 2600 SZ was always a rarefied and expensive product. With a list price of 3,970,000 lire, it was almost twice as costly as a Giulia GT and about 30% more than a 2600 Sprint. It should not be entirely unsurprising, then, that only 105 examples were ever built.

Pininfarina's 2600-based coupé Speciale of 1963 prefigured its forthcoming Duetto.

PININFARINA'S SPECIALES

Pininfarina designed two Alfa 2600-based concept cars: the 2600 Cabriolet Speciale (which debuted at the Turin Show in 1962) and the 2600 Coupé Speciale (at the 1963 Brussels Show). While the designs may have looked a lot like other contemporary Pininfarina shapes, they were certainly elegant, in some ways prefiguring Pininfarina's forthcoming design for the Duetto (see Chapter 5). *Quattroruote* magazine was certainly enthusiastic about the design's "balanced mass, harmonious curves with design by the hand of the master". There were reportedly plans to turn these designs into proper production models, but alas that never happened.

Chapter Four

GIULIETTA TIPO 750 & 101:
NEW HORIZONS

While the Alfa Romeo 1900 had pioneered the idea of a mass-produced car for the Milanese company, it was still too large and too expensive for the average customer in post-war Italy. The true "people's Alfa" would be the all-new Giulietta that was launched in 1954. The "popular" claim was fully justified: over 157,000 Giuliettas would be sold over the model's lifetime, firmly establishing Alfa Romeo as a volume car manufacturer for the first time in its history.

The Giulietta Tipo 750 family was the brainchild of engineer Orazio Satta Puliga. In his talented team were Giuseppe Busso (responsible for the powertrain) and Ivo Colucci (who was behind the chassis). Like the 1900, the Giulietta had monocoque construction, independent front suspension by double wishbones, coil-over dampers and a rigid rear axle. However, the rear end was more sophisticated, evolving to a more substantial A-frame, still suspended by coil springs.

To fund the Giulietta project, Alfa Romeo had issued security bonds with a promise that 200 bond holders would win one of the new cars on its launch, which was due to be in 1953. However, that date passed and both investors and the Italian press started

The sporting Giulietta family together: SZ, Spider and Sprint coupé.

The 1955 Giulietta Berlina marked another move towards the mass market, but signally retained Alfa's engineering integrity.

This is a prototype of the Giulietta Sprint, featuring a lifting hatchback that didn't make production.

at the same time successfully appeasing investors. However, it would not be until 1955 that the Sprint entered production, while the four-door Giulietta Berlina would not start to come off the lines until 1956, following its April 1955 debut at the Turin Show.

As for the Giulietta Spider, that debuted just after the Berlina saloon, with the definitive production version arriving in autumn 1955. While Bertone's styling for the Sprint was a tough act to follow, Pinin Farina's lines for the Spider were equally well received.

The engine was a brand new twin-cam 1290cc four-cylinder unit which benefited from an unprecedented amount of aluminium in its construction. The engine was designed by Giuseppe Busso, whose penchant for weight containment derived directly from his years as an aviation engine designer. The saloon started with a 53hp 1290cc engine but from 1957, the TI (Turismo Internazionale) version raised that to 65hp. The second series Giulietta (Tipo 101) was launched at the 1959 Frankfurt Motor Show with a few updates. The third series Giulietta arrived in autumn 1961 with uprated engines and exhausts seeing power rise to 62hp, or 74hp in TI guise. When the new Giulia 1600 saloon arrived in June 1962, the old Giulietta Berlina continued alongside it until 1963, and until 1965 in TI form.

As for the choice of the name Giulietta, that speaks for itself – for what is Romeo without his Giulietta? Meanwhile, the long line of celebrity owners queuing to buy one, including Sophia Loren, Gina Lollobrigida and Diana Dors, helped make the Giulietta a star itself.

to express nervousness. There was considerable pressure on the man whose job it was to bring the new car to production: ex-Porsche man, Rudolf Hruska. Among the many challenges he faced was the fact that the four-door bodyshell produced an unpleasant throbbing sound in the cabin at speed, which was just one of several reasons why its launch was delayed.

With an urgent need to come up with something quickly, Alfa Romeo took the highly unusual step of launching the Giulietta in Sprint (coupé) form before the Berlina (saloon). This was frankly a hastily prepared debut, but the audacious move worked. The Giulietta Sprint was triumphantly unveiled at the April 1954 Turin Motor Show, to huge acclaim,

GIULIETTA SPRINT (1954-1962)
& GIULIA SPRINT (1962-1965)

The Sprint's shape was a triumph for Nuccio Bertone's carrozzeria. It was not strictly speaking the work of one man. The initial configuration was by Giuseppe Scarnati of Alfa Romeo but his design was not especially liked by the management, so Mario Boano of Ghia and Franco Scaglione of Bertone were called in to collaborate on the first prototype. Boano soon moved on, and it was left to be completed by 37-year old Scaglione, to whom the design is usually rightly attributed.

Elegantly simple, well proportioned and understated, this was without question one of the best coupé designs of the 1950s, and it has withstood changing fashions over time with perfect grace. The front end echoed Bertone's 1900 Sprint, with air intakes either side of the grille, like moustaches, but it had its definite character. The car's remarkable aerodynamics also made it superbly suited to high-speed competition at events like the Mille Miglia.

Central to the appeal of the new range was its fabulous 1290cc twin-overhead camshaft engine, derived from the Alfa 1900. Both the block and head were made out of aluminium (a pioneering advance for a road car), and the gearbox and differential casing were aluminium, too; the cylinder liners were of cast iron. There were twin overhead camshafts, unique for such a small engine at the time, and the crankshaft was mounted on five bearings. In the coupé, the 1.3-litre unit initially developed 65hp at

6000rpm, rising to 79hp from 1958 – in both cases usefully more than the saloon. With its light overall weight and lively engine, all versions of the Sprint could exceed 100mph.

As with the 1900, the four-speed gearbox initially had a steering column change (it would be several years before a floor-mounted gear change was used). With its all-independent suspension consisting of coil springs, wishbones and anti-roll bar up front, and coil springs, upper wishbones and struts at the rear, the handling was far more sporting than the average car

The Giulietta Sprint has an undeniable grace of design. Franco Scaglione's shape has become a truly timeless classic.

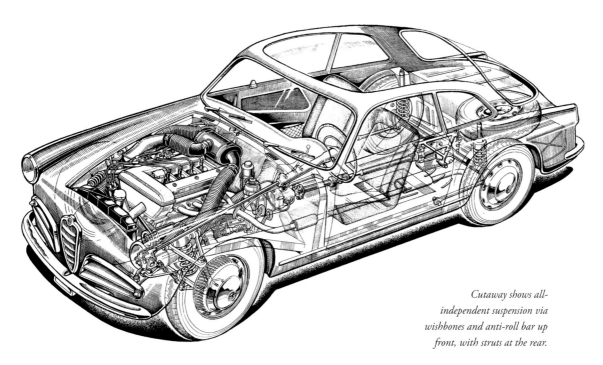

Cutaway shows all-independent suspension via wishbones and anti-roll bar up front, with struts at the rear.

The Sprint always looked like a completely different model from the Giulietta Berlina.

In action, the Sprint lived up to its name, even with a mere 65hp in its original spec.

of the 1950s. That encouraged drivers to campaign it competitively on race tracks and in rallies, and although there was some criticism of the degree of body roll in corners, it rode very comfortably. Braking was by drums all round.

Inside, it was a 2+2 rather than a full four-seater,

and the instrumentation was unusually generous for the period. The steel dashboard included a speedometer, rev counter, oil pressure gauge and oil temperature gauge, fuel level gauge and water temperature gauge. What would have been a pioneering feature – a lifting hatchback, as seen on the prototype – was replaced in production by a conventional boot lid.

A range of options included a set of suitcases designed for the rear seat area, fog lamps, radio, imitation leather dashboard, leather seat upholstery and an aluminium steering wheel with a wooden rim. When the customer chose any of these options, the car received a chrome ring in the boot-mounted Alfa Romeo badge.

SPECIFICATIONS	
GIULIETTA SPRINT SERIES 1/SERIES 2	
Engine:	1290cc four-cyl twin-cam
Power:	65hp @ 6000rpm/79hp @ 6300rpm
Torque:	108Nm (80lb ft) @ 4000rpm
	98Nm (72lb ft) @ 3600rpm
Transmission:	4-speed manual
Wheels:	15in steel
Weight:	880kg/935kg
Max speed:	102mph/106mph
0-62mph	13.2sec/12.5sec

Early Giulietta Sprints had small rear light clusters and a simpler shape.

Bertone was tasked with producing the new car. Initially, the company had to call on panel beaters at various small Turin workshops to do this. A mere 12 units were registered in 1954, each one differing slightly. The launch price was more than 1,700,000 lire – cheaper than most sports cars but still well out of the reach of the average worker, whose average monthly salary at the time was 40,000 lire. In time, Bertone accepted that he needed to expand and built a new plant at his Grugliasco base on the outskirts of Turin, turning a body shop into a factory.

In June 1958, the Giulietta Sprint Series 2 was presented at the Monza racetrack. This would bear the chassis Tipo prefix 101 rather than 750. Power rose from 65hp to 79hp, courtesy of a higher 8.5:1

Over 24,084 Sprints were built between 1954 and 1965.

Cabin offered seating for two plus two passengers, and a well-equipped dashboard.

S P E C I F I C A T I O N S	
GIULIA 1600 SPRINT	
Engine:	1570cc four-cyl twin-cam
Power:	91hp @ 6200rpm
Torque:	147Nm (108lb ft) @ 3700rpm
Transmission:	5-speed manual
Wheels:	15in steel
Weight:	975kg
Top speed:	106mph
0-62mph:	10.2sec

Renamed Giulia 1600 Sprint in 1962, the coupé's essential shape altered very little.

compression ratio, new exhaust manifolds, stronger cylinder block and bigger valves. Other mechanical changes included a far superior floor-mounted gear lever and new Porsche-type synchromesh in the gearbox, while the fuel pump was moved to a lower position.

Bertone's elegant bodywork didn't change much, but the front end was restyled with new chrome-framed mesh grilles, larger headlamps, extra side indicators and larger tail lights on vestigial fins, which replaced the earlier rounded rear wings. The interior was improved and a redesigned dashboard now incor-

porated a strip speedometer.

The Sprint's "handcrafted" era came to end in the summer of 1960, when Bertone opened his new plant in Grugliasco, where bodies would now be assembled using electric spot welding.

One might have expected the Giulietta Sprint to be axed when the new Tipo 105 Giulia arrived in 1962, but Alfa Romeo decided to continue offering the 101 Sprint, although they somewhat confusingly rebadged it as a Giulia. While the styling hardly altered, the big change was the installation of the 1570cc engine from the Giulia range – hence

Side profile shows off superb proportions to best effect.

Later models had larger tail light clusters.

1600 Sprint died in 1964 but a 1.3-litre version was revived for one further year.

The old 1290cc engine gave way to a 1570cc unit in the Giulia 1600 Sprint.

the new model was called Giulia 1600 Sprint. With 91hp of power at 6200rpm and 108lb ft of torque at 3700rpm, it had usefully better performance than the outgoing 1290cc version, helped by the adoption of Alfa's five-speed gearbox as standard. Inside, the dashboard received a fresh look with new instruments and a revised dash panel. Drum brakes were fitted front and rear until 1964, at which point discs arrived up front. However, the 1600 Sprint would be withdrawn later in 1964, after some 7107 examples had been made. That wasn't quite the end of the Sprint story, though. Alfa Romeo reintroduced a 1290cc model in 1964, under the name 1300 Sprint, which lasted in production for one more year, during which time over 1800 were made.

Both affordable and useable, the Sprint proved a very popular choice with buyers. Between 1954 and 1965, some 24,084 examples were built in all.

GIULIETTA SPRINT VELOCE (1956-1962)

The Sprint had considerable appeal in motorsport. However, its potential was being challenged by Porsche's new models. Alfa Romeo desperately needed a model to do battle in races like the Mille Miglia and Targa Florio. The company's Oratio Satta Puliga was inspired to ask Giuseppe Busso to develop an upgraded version in 1956. The Alleggerita, or lightened, Sprint Veloce (SV) was the result. As well as

extra power from the 1290cc twin-cam engine, the SV made great strides in cutting weight.

Bertone built all early Sprints by hand. To make a Sprint Veloce, Bertone took a standard steel tub and removed it to a separate sub-assembly line. Aluminium was used in place of steel for the doors, bonnet and boot lid. Much of the steel and chrome trim was replaced by aluminium, too, such as the bumpers and body trim. The regular glass windows were swapped

Sprint Veloce (SV) Alleggerita ("lightened") shed a huge amount of weight compared to the standard Sprint.

Aluminium opening panels and trim, plus Plexiglas windows, all helped to reduce weight.

Hollowed-out door skins and thinner front seats marked out the focused SV.

The Sprint Veloce is a rare and, today, highly desirable variant.

for lightweight Plexiglas at the sides and rear, and the winding side windows were replaced by sliding items. While the plastic windows themselves didn't save much weight, doing away with the winding mechanisms certainly did, and allowed lighter "hollowed out" door skins. The front seats had thinner bases, while the rear seat was removed for a flat shelf to be fitted

– ideal for spare tyres and parts. Much of the sound deadening was stripped out, too, while the choke knob and glove box lid were also deleted. The weight saving was in the order of 100kg, the SV weighing just 780kg overall (unladen).

The Sprint Veloce's 1290cc engines were hand-assembled with closer tolerances, lightened pistons,

special cams and ignition timing, sand-cast Weber 40DCO3 carburettors and a magnesium oil pan and intake manifold. The result was a power output of 79hp at 6500rpm. The standard Sprint final drive was changed from 9/41 to 10/41, which gave it a slightly higher top speed of 106mph. A larger fuel tank (84 litres versus 56) also enabled longer touring distances. The car did well in competition, notably sweeping the board in the extremely wet 1956 Mille Miglia,

finishing 1-2-3 in class and 11-12-15 overall.

The Veloce was distinguished by its extra 'E' stamped by hand on the chassis plate – hence the 750E moniker often used for these cars. As few as 600 first series models were made up until 1958. Alfa Romeo had also produced, from September 1957, a "touring" version of the Veloce called the Confortevole ("comfortable"), which combined the Series 1 Sprint specification with the mechanicals of the Veloce, and was recognisable by its Perspex winding windows in aluminium frames and larger headlamps. Around 200 Confortevoles were made.

In 1958, the Sprint Veloce was updated to become the Series 2, sharing the same aesthetic improvements as the regular Sprint. However it no longer with benefited from lighter bodywork, and weight increased by a substantial 190kg to 970kg. To compensate, the engine was given a higher compression ratio to boost power from 79hp to 96hp, resulting in a top speed now up to 108mph. The Sprint Speciale's five-speed gearbox could now be fitted as an extra-cost option, too. Some 3058 examples of the second series Sprint Veloce were made by the time production ended in 1962.

Extra power enhanced the SV's speed and it notably finished 1-2-3 in its class at the 1956 Mille Miglia.

SPECIFICATIONS

SPRINT VELOCE SERIES 1/SERIES 2

Engine:	1290cc 4-cyl twin-cam
Power	79hp @ 6500rpm/96hp @ 6500rpm
Torque	108Nm (80lb ft) @ 5500rpm
Transmission	4-speed manual
	(5-speed option from 1958)
Wheels	15in steel
Weight	780kg/970kg
Max speed	106mph/108mph
0-62mph	10.9sec/10.0sec

Pinin Farina's convertibel shape was every bit as alluring as Bertone's coupé.

GIULIETTA SPIDER (1955-1962)
& GIULIA 1600 SPIDER (1962-1965)

The impetus for an open-topped version of the new Giulietta came from Max Hoffman, Alfa Romeo's US importer, who knew that such a model would sell very well in his home market. Alfa Romeo turned not to Bertone when it came to creating a Spider version of the 101 Giulietta, but to Pinin Farina; this "sharing out" of body styles was a well established Alfa custom by now. If Farina had been concerned that

In 1959, the 1290cc engine was boosted to 79hp for the regular model and 96hp in the 1570cc Veloce.

its work would suffer by comparison with Bertone's lauded coupé, it needn't have worried; the open-top two-seater realised by Pinin Farina was achingly beautiful, so much so that it became known as, "La piu amata degli italiani" or "the Italians' Favourite". In time, Pinin Farina himself would call it, "a signorina that never ages". There were comparisons with Farina's shapes for the Lancia Aurelia B24 Spider, leading some to call the Alfa the "poor man's Aurelia". Every part of the bodywork was different from the

Some likened the Alfa to a poor man's Lancia Aurelia Spider.

Interior was strictly for two people, simply and elegantly trimmed, as ever with Alfa.

The 1955 Giulietta Spider, seen here in prototype form (and now on display at the Alfa Romeo Museum).

SPECIFICATIONS

GIULIETTA SPIDER SERIES 1/SERIES 2

Engine:	1290cc four-cyl twin-cam
Power:	65hp @ 6000rpm/79hp @ 6300rpm
Torque:	108Nm (80lb ft) @ 4000rpm
	/98Nm (72lb ft) @ 3600rpm
Transmission:	4-speed manual
Wheels:	15in steel
Weight:	860kg/930kg
Max speed:	96mph/98mph
0-62mph:	12.7sec/11.8sec

Sprint coupé's, and the wheelbase was shorter, too, at 2200mm versus 2380mm.

As with the Sprint, the Spider was powered by Alfa's 65hp 1290cc engine. It must be said that performance lagged slightly behind the Sprint, though, as a result of poorer aerodynamics. The 1956 arrival of the Spider Veloce with its twin-Weber carburetthp engine certainly helped its sports car credentials – although the Spider never got the Sprint SV's Alleggerita treatment.

The Spider debuted just after the Berlina saloon in Milan in the spring of 1955, although it took until the Paris Show of autumn 1955 for the definitive production version to arrive. Pinin Farina took on production of the Spider, the very first model to be mass-produced in series at its Turin plant. The model proved very successful, being especially popular in the USA, even though it was comparatively expensive.

A second series Spider arrived in 1959, with the same boosts in power as the Sprint: 79hp for the regular model and 96hp for the Veloce. In addition, the wheelbase was extended to 2250mm. In 1961 came the third series with lightly revised bodywork and interior. The most obvious changes were bigger rear lights and a lower rear wing line, while better interior appointments made it more comfortable.

When the 105 Giulia arrived in 1962, the Spider was upgraded to 1570cc twin-cam power and renamed the Giulia 1600 Spider. That svelte two-seater Spider body retained its shape intact, but now there was a

The Spider's wheelbase was shorter than the Sprint's, lending it more dynamic immediacy.

raised bonnet to accommodate the taller block of the longer-stroke 1.6 engine. In the changeover, the Spider also gained a five-speed gearbox, a set of disc front brakes and an improved suspension set-up. There was also more power, now up to 91hp. The twin-carb Giulia Spider Veloce was launched in 1964, offering an even racier 112hp, and its taller final drive ratio helped give it a higher top speed, at 112mph versus 106mph.

Some 14,300 Giulietta Spiders were built from 1955 to 1962, plus a further 2796 Veloce versions. From 1962 to 1965, the Giulia 1600 Spider reached 9250 and the Veloce model 1091. Totting it all up, that made a grand total of 27,437 Spiders in all.

Like the Sprint, the Spider evolved to Giulia 1600 form in 1962.

S P E C I F I C A T I O N S	
GIULIETTA SPIDER VELOCE	
SERIES 1/SERIES 2	
Engine:	1290cc four-cyl twin-cam
Power:	79hp @ 6500rpm/96hp @ 6500rpm
Torque:	118Nm (87lb ft) @ 5300rpm
	108Nm (80lb ft) @ 5500rpm
Transmission:	4-speed manual
Wheels:	15in steel
Weight:	865kg/935kg
Max speed:	106mph/108mph
0-62mph:	11.8sec/11sec

S P E C I F I C A T I O N S	
GIULIA 1600 SPIDER	
/1600 SPIDER VELOCE	
Engine:	1570cc four-cyl twin-cam
Power:	91hp @ 6200rpm/113hp @ 6500rpm
Torque:	147Nm (108lb ft) @ 3700rpm
	/127Nm (94lb ft) @ 4200rpm
Transmission:	5-speed manual
Wheels:	15in steel
Weight:	960kg
Top speed:	106mph/112mph
0-62mph:	11sec/10.2sec

The 1590cc engine of the Giulia 1600 Spider developed up to 112hp in Veloce tune.

Only a few aesthetic changes marked later models from early ones.

GIULIETTA & GIULIA SPRINT SPECIALE (1957-1965)

Few cars have ever looked so dramatic as the Giulietta Sprint Speciale. Perhaps that should not have been surprising, since it was the work of one of the greatest maverick designers ever to come out of Italy, Franco Scaglione. His initial ambition to become an aircraft aerodynamicist were thwarted by post-war restrictions on aircraft building in Italy, so instead he joined Bertone, where he went on to become chief designer in 1951. While at Bertone, he created three very special Berlinetta Aerodinamica Tecnica (BAT) prototypes in 1953-1955 and continued his aerodynamic studies with the Alfa Romeo Sportiva prototypes (see Chapter 2). Scaglione was also largely responsible for the Giulietta Sprint's design.

The story of the Sprint Speciale, however, begins not at Bertone but Zagato. Alfa Romeo had seen how successful Zagato's rebodied 1290cc Giulietta Sprint Veloce Zagato (SVZ) had been in racing, so Alfa asked Bertone to produce a lightweight, aerodynamic coupé that could compete with it on track, as well as in the showroom. Internally, Bertone dubbed this new project Sprint Spinta ("tuned Sprint").

Scaglione used as a basis a shortened and lowered Giulietta Spider chassis. He designed a grille-less nose and tail that were notably tapered to reduce drag and promote high-speed stability, and the prototype was widely photographed on the Milan-Turin autostrada, covered in wool tufts. Reputedly its drag coefficient was just 0.28.

Alfa's new coupé was initially presented as the Giulietta Speciale at the Turin Show in October 1957. A second prototype, with a shortened nose and raised roofline, appeared at the Geneva Show in March 1958, while a third prototype with a proper Alfa grille appeared at the Turin Salon later in 1958. So far the car had been presented with aluminium bodywork, with the bonnet, boot and doors realised in a special

The Giulietta Sprint Speciale was designed, like the Sprint, by Franco Scaglione.

Quirky design features abounded, such as the transparent deflector ahead of the windscreen.

The slippery shape of the SS lent it a reputed drag coefficient of just 0.28.

Launched as a Giulietta, the Sprint Speciale evolved to Giulia spec and 1.6-litre power in 1962.

non-deformable aluminium called Titonal. Plexiglas side and rear screens helped save weight, too, but the 780kg Speciale still ended up being 65kg heavier than the SVZ.

When the final production model – now dubbed Sprint Speciale, or simply SS to many enthusiasts – was presented in June 1959 at Monza, it had been redesigned once again with a less swooping tail and a higher roofline, while the whole thing was six inches shorter. It now had steel bodywork with an aluminium bonnet, boot and doors, plus Plexiglas screens – but it had also gained weight, now weighing over a tonne. One notable quirk was a translucent baffle mounted just ahead of the windscreen, designed to keep the wipers in place at speed.

The 1290cc engine developed a healthy 97hp thanks to balanced rods and pistons, a 9.7:1 compression ratio and twin Weber carburettors. Its ability to achieve very high speeds with a 1.3-litre powerplant

was exceptional; indeed *Autosport* magazine managed to tease 124mph out of an early "low-nose" model in its 1960 road test. The SS boasted a five-speed gearbox with a floor-mounted lever, and slotted in as the sportiest model in Alfa's range at its launch. However, the Sprint Speciale ended up being "repurposed" in the market; Alfa conceded that Zagato's approach was superior for racing and let Zagato develop the Giulietta SZ (see below). The Sprint Speciale was thus sold as an upmarket grand touring car with a plushly trimmed interior.

Autosport's road test described the SS as "competition bred and from a long line of racing machines... a small-capacity machine of such refinement and performance." *Road & Track* magazine in the US described it as "an exquisite jewel beyond comparison or price" – although of course it did have a price, and a very high one at that (as much as an Aston Martin DB3 in the UK).

The SS was never campaigned much in competition; here is one racing in Marrakech, Morocco.

Interior was much plusher than originally planned, as it switched roles from racer to grand tourer.

In early 1960 came the second series Sprint Speciale with its nose panel and headlights raised by 70mm (so that it satisfied US regulations), plus front bumpers added. At the rear, the bootlid was extended to the lip of a deeper Kamm tail, which incorporated stacked twin rear lights. The doors were now of steel, as were trim items which had previously been aluminium, while the windows were now glass. The upholstery was upgraded in the style of the Giulietta Sprint, too.

In this form, the Sprint Speciale was sadly even heavier. The SS had frankly taken too long to reach proper production and was too expensive. Bertone built the SS at its Grugliasco factory, and when production ceased in 1962, only 1252 second series cars had been produced, with perhaps 100 examples prior to that.

Alfa's new Giulia Tipo 105 range was launched in 1962 and the new 1570cc engine was duly shoe-horned into the Sprint Speciale in 1963, the model being renamed Giulia Sprint Speciale. The 1.6-litre powerplant had 112hp in the SS thanks to a high compression ratio and twin Weber carburettors. It was altogether a much more flexible engine, even if it yielded no better performance figures, since the car weighed 75kg more. Comfort was improved, too, notably with a new dashboard. In 1964, front drum brakes were replaced by discs.

The Giulia SS overlapped the new Giulia Sprint GT (see next chapter) but always remained higher up in Alfa's range. Some 1400 examples of the Giulia SS had been made by the end of production in 1965, with no direct replacement following.

Long tail was designed to reduce drag and boost high-speed stability

SPECIFICATIONS

GIULIETTA/GIULIA SPRINT SPECIALE

Engine:	1290cc/1570cc four-cyl twin-cam
Power:	97hp @ 6500rpm
	/112hp @ 6500rpm
Torque:	130Nm (96lb ft) @ 5500rpm
	131Nm (97lb ft) @ 4200rpm
Transmission:	5-speed manual
Wheels:	15in steel
Weight:	1110kg/1185kg
Top speed:	114mph/119mph
0-62mph:	10.3sec

The Giulietta Sprint Veloce Zagato was not an official Alfa but had special significance because it inspired the later SZ.

With its light weight, the SVZ was a far better performer than Alfa's own Sprint Speciale.

GIULIETTA SPRINT VELOCE ZAGATO (1956-1959)

While it was never an official Alfa Romeo model, the Giulietta Sprint Veloce Zagato (or SVZ) is definitely worthy of mention in this book because its success directly gave birth to a model that was an official Alfa: the SZ (for which see below).

The birth of the SVZ had its origins in an accident at the 1956 Mille Miglia. When two brothers – Carlo and Dore Leto di Priolo – crashed their Giulietta Sprint Veloce, the car was judged beyond repair. As a result, it was taken to Elio Zagato, who dismounted the mechanicals, put

them in a Zagato-built tubular frame and then constructed a new body around it all, designed by Gianni Zagato. The new car was still recognisably a Giulietta Sprint Veloce but it differed enough for it to receive a new name in race programmes: Sprint Veloce Zagato.

Zagato's car was far lighter than the SV – 110kg less, in fact – and therefore far faster. At the car's debut at Monza in September 1956, Massimo Leto di Priolo beat regular Sprint Veloces hands down. The car's advantages were crystal clear, and there was suddenly a clamouring throng of racing drivers knocking at Zagato's door. Zagato wisely decided to

The Giulietta SZ borrowed the SS chassis but it was much lighter and more focused.

update the design and offer it to the public.

Through 1957, three or four further cars were converted with "double-bubble" roofs. In 1958-1959, Zagato produced a further 14 SVZs with a more developed design that definitively broke away from the Bertone shape: the nose was flatter, the roof lower and the tail shorter and more rounded. The SVZ was very much a coachbuilt car, not an official model. If you wanted one, you had to buy a brand new Sprint Veloce, then get Zagato to chop it up and rebuild it as an SVZ. As a result it was exceedingly expensive, but with racing success awaiting buyers, it was worth the outlay for many.

GIULIETTA SZ (1960-1962)

Alfa Romeo paid close attention to Zagato's efforts with the SVZ, and eventually decided to sanction a new, official model designed and built by Zagato. Alfa agreed to supply Zagato with the short wheelbase Giulietta Sprint Speciale chassis for it to create the new SZ (Sprint Zagato).

While the Sprint Speciale's chief characteristic was aerodynamic efficiency, the SZ not only had a smooth shape but was also an extremely lightweight machine; unladen, it weighed a mere 854kg, almost 100kg less than the SS, mostly thanks to the fact that its bodywork was made of aluminium over a light tubular

As launched, the SZ had a rounded rear end.

The SVZ was a racing star; here Pasquier tackles an Alpine pass in 1960.

The SZ had clear dynamic advantages over the SS: it was essentially a racer for the road.

Mechanically, the SZ duplicated the SS's spec: 97hp engine and five-speed gearbox.

Ideally suited to competition the SZ scored many victories. Here it is on the 1963 Alpine Rally.

frame, with Plexiglas windows and Campagnolo alloy wheels. As a result, the SZ was ideally suited to competition work.

This was a strict two-seater, whose Spartan interior was minimally trimmed. To keep weight down, it had a glassfibre dashboard, skimpy seats and very light doors. Mechanically, it duplicated the specification of the Sprint Speciale, complete with its 97hp engine and five-speed gearbox. To drive, the SZ was essentially a barely-contained race car, with more agile handling than any other Giulietta model, flat cornering behaviour and sharp steering, although

The 1961 second series SZ was altered by Ercole Spada to lengthen it both front and rear.

The severely cut-off tail gave the revised SZ its nickname of "coda tronca".

it did acquire a reputation for being somewhat twitchy in the wet. It was hardly a refined cruising machine, either.

Compared to the larger SS, the 1960 SZ's shape was stubbier and more rounded, as well as shorter, narrower and lower than the SS, with headlamps faired in behind glass covers. In 1961 came the second series, which adopted the aerodynamic theories of Ercole Spada, then newly arrived at Zagato, who had been heavily influenced by the aerodynamicist Wunibald Kamm. Spada lengthened the body front and rear so that the overall length rose by 150mm, while height dropped from 1250mm to 1230mm. The tail now tapered down at a gentler angle, flowing via a wraparound rear window before culminating in a distinctly cut-off tail – coda tronca in Italian – designed to bring aerodynamic and weight-saving benefits. Indeed, the second series SZ weighed 14kg less at 840kg unladen. Disc brakes were adopted at the front end, too. The new car was

certainly quicker – one was timed on the Mulsanne Straight at Le Mans doing 220km/h (137mph).

Being a hand-built car, its price was high (2,875,000 lire) and as a result only 217 examples of the SZ were made up until 1962. Today it is regarded as one of Alfa Romeo's most prestigious post-war models, and avidly sought after by collectors.

SPECIFICATIONS	
GIULIETTA SZ SERIES 1/SERIES 2	
Engine:	1290cc four-cyl twin-cam
Power:	97hp @ 6500rpm
Torque:	130Nm (96lb ft) @ 5500rpm
Transmission:	5-speed manual
Wheels:	15in alloy
Weight:	854kg/840kg
Top speed:	124mph/137mph
0-62mph:	9.5sec

Chapter Five

TIPO 105 & 115:
HIGH ASPIRATIONS

The Giulia Berlina was produced from 1962 to 1978. Pictured here is a TI Super saloon.

When Alfa Romeo started considering a replacement for its lauded Giulietta saloon, it initially contemplated merely updating the styling and fitting a larger 1.6-litre engine. However, this was quickly rejected for a more radically different model: the Tipo 105 Giulia. This would be a much larger car than the Giulietta: its longer wheelbase resulted in a car that was substantially longer, and wider, too, giving it a bigger cabin into the bargain.

The Giulia saloon was presented to the press at Monza circuit on 27 June 1962. Broadly speaking, its mechanical layout was inherited from the Giulietta. The double wishbone front suspension was improved with new links and there was a front anti-roll bar. At the rear, the live axle format was retained but the struts were now made of box-section steel and mounted lower down. Meanwhile the steering box was now mounted behind the axle line.

Power came from a new 1570cc version of Alfa's twin-cam engine, the extra capacity deriving from a deeper engine block that permitted a longer stroke. Other changes included Solex carburation, a two-part exhaust manifold and an aluminium sump. In the TI

saloon as launched, the 1.6 engine boasted 90hp, or 113hp in TI Super guise. In 1964 Alfa added a 1300 saloon which used the old 1290cc engine with 80hp.

The gearbox was a sophisticated five-speed manual with a floor-mounted lever, and the differential housing was in aluminium to reduce weight. Drum brakes inherited from the Giulietta Sprint Veloce were replaced very early in the model's life; even the saloon quickly got all-round disc brakes. This was pretty exotic: in the mid-1960s four-wheel disc brakes were still the territory of racing cars and Ferraris, and the discs measured a sizeable 10.5in (267mm) at the front and 9.75in (248mm) at the back.

Alfa's engineering genius, Ivo Colucci, developed the new Giulia 105 with help from Turin Polytechnic's advanced wind tunnel. The extensive aerodynamic development gave rise to Alfa publicising the new car as "the automobile designed by the wind". It didn't necessarily look slippery – "Like how aerodynamic can a brick be?" remarked Sports Car Graphic magazine – but Alfa Romeo claimed a Cd figure of 0.34, which was very low for the time.

The Giulia was an unmitigated triumph for Alfa Romeo: not only was it well received by the press and public, it emerged as a very strong seller. It was also highly successful in motorsport. The Tipo 105 spawned a whole multitude of variations over the next decade, the first of which was the Bertone-designed Giulia Sprint GT coupé in 1963, one of the prettiest shapes of its era. This was closely followed by the new Spider of 1966, initially called the Duetto, which was another iconic design of the era, this time by Pininfarina.

The next step in the development of the Giulia family was the 1750 engine – actually 1779cc – announced in January 1968. The faithful 1750 twin-cam was duly fitted into pretty much the whole Giulia range, from saloon to Spider.

The final incarnation of the Giulia came in 1971 with the adoption, right across the range (saloon, coupé and Spider), of a 1962cc version of the twin-cam four, marketed as "2000". The reason why the 1750 engine only lasted for two-and-a-half years was down to the Italian domestic tax regime, which classed the 1779cc powerplant in the same category as 2.0-litre cars; Alfa Romeo had simply not been bold enough to go up to 2.0 litres in the first place, which it addressed with the more potent bored-out 1962cc unit. This gradually evolved over the years, gaining fuel injection, a catalytic converter and variable valve timing. Alfa also continued fitting 1300 and 1600 engines into saloons, Spiders and Sprints, using the "Junior" badge for these models.

Carrozzeria Zagato made two official Giulia variants. The first was a tongue-in-cheek pre-war 1750 lookalike, instigated by the Italian motoring magazine *Quattroruote*. The so-called Gran Sport 4R was offered for sale from 1966. Zagato also built the quirky Junior Z coupé on the Spider platform between 1969 and 1975.

The Tipo 105 chassis prefix was upgraded to Tipo 115 from 1972, although some Giulia-family models did not adopt the chassis designation until several years later. While the Alfetta of 1972 effectively replaced the Giulia as Alfa's mid-sized saloon offering, the well-liked older model continued going as the Nuova Giulia (saloon) and the Sprint (coupé), both with 1290cc power only, continuing right up until 1978. But the Giulia platform had a life that would last far longer than this: the Giulia-based Spider would not finally bow out until 1994. Evolution was the key. The shape evolved with a cut-off Kamm tail in 1969 and major redesigns by Pininfarina in 1983 and 1990. Controversy surrounded some of the Spider evolutions – the bespoilered treatment of American cars and the 1980s Spiders in particular – but the essence of the original Spider was preserved throughout.

The fact that so little was altered to the 105/115's underpinnings during its lifespan says much about how advanced it was at launch, with its five-speed gearbox, four-wheel disc brakes and all-alloy engine. Although its suspension layout of a live rear axle was never state-of-the-art, the innately correct chassis geometry produced handling that was the equal of any independently-sprung rival.

While the Giulia, coupé and Spider are quintessentially Italian products, made in Alfa's factories (or, in the Spider's case, at Pininfarina), some models were also assembled abroad. For instance, Alfa Romeo Sudafrica assembled various models at its plant in Johannesburg, including the Giulia Super, GT Junior and GTV.

After a career spanning almost 30 years – one of the longest of any car, let alone in the faddishly fashionable world of sports cars – the 105 era came to an end in 1994 when the Spider was retired. The total number of Giulia 105 coupés built from 1963 to 1976 was 225,215, plus an additional 998 GTC convertibles, making this one of the most successful two-door cars of the era. When you add in a total of 124,104 Spiders built between 1966 and 1994, it's easy to appreciate what an impact this generation of Alfa Romeo had in the marketplace, and why it remains such a numerous and popular car among enthusiasts today.

As launched in 1963, the Giulia Sprint GT had a pure, unfussy appearance.

GIULIA SPRINT GT (1963-1968)

By the time Bertone was given the go-ahead to design the replacement for the Giulietta Sprint, its star designer, Giorgetto Giugiaro, already familiar to Alfa for designing the 2000 Sprint coupé, was absent. In 1960 Giugiaro had been spirited away by government decree, billeted in army barracks to perform his compulsory national service. Bertone was not going to lose such a man without a fight, however, and succeeded in pulling enough strings to allow the young designer to live in a hotel, rather than barracks, giving him a suitable base from which to work on the new Alfa Romeo design project.

The earlier Alfa Romeo 2000 Sprint that Giugiaro had designed (see Chapter 3) clearly influenced his smaller Giulia Sprint, and he completed the basic design work in the spring of 1960. The 2350mm wheelbase – some 160mm shorter than the saloon's

Bertone's Giulia Sprint GT became one of Alfa Romeo's most iconic models.

and 30mm shorter than the old Giulietta Sprint's – helped him to obtain perfect proportions for his newcomer.

Alfa Romeo was so impressed with the design that it pushed ahead with it with absolutely no changes. The clean design featured an unbroken waistline styling crease, falling slightly as it reached the neat tail, which gave the car fantastic balance and a sense of integration that few rivals could muster. Impressively refined details included recessed door handles and inset headlamps. Early cars featured a curious raised front bonnet edge, giving the engine bay an additional cooling air intake, which gave rise to the car's Italian nickname "scalino" (step front).

Inside, there was seating for four, or perhaps more accurately 2+2. The fascia was simple and functional, but featured the luxury of many more dials than was typical for the era. Right-hand drive finally became available with this model (the Giulietta Sprint had been left-hook only) so exports to the UK, Australia and elsewhere were much more buoyant.

Mechanically, the 1600 Sprint GT used the 1570cc engine from the Giulia TI saloon but it was tuned slightly by using two Weber carburettors to raise the power from 90hp to 103hp at 6000rpm. Together with less weight than the saloon, that gave it a healthy top speed of 111mph.

The handling was widely praised in press reports. *Road & Track* said: "In a fast corner, the car is basically neutral… As one enters a turn at speed, there is a certain amount of roll oversteer initially… but as soon as the car is positioned, this changes abruptly and the car becomes extremely stable." It also concluded that

Giugiaro designed the Sprint GT while he was on national service in the Italian army.

this was, "a driver's car in the Alfa tradition" and able "to cover ground quickly and without effort… impossible to find fault with the gearbox… [For] those people who doubt racing improves the breed, the Giulia Sprint GT proves conclusively that it docs."

It was in late 1963 – well over three years after Giugiaro had designed the car – that the Giulia Sprint GT was finally unveiled at Alfa's new factory at Arese in Milan, which had been built to expand the company's production capacity. The coupé would be the very first car assembled here, although its mechanicals were still built at the old Portello works.

Some 22,671 examples of the 1600 Sprint GT were made up until 1966, by which time the hotter Giulia 1600 Sprint GT Veloce had already been launched (it

The so-called "scalino" (step front) raised bonnet line is clear to see in this image.

In 1965 Sprint GT Veloce (GTV) guise, the coupé had elevated performance (top speed of 116mph).

Road testers reckoned the GTV was much more than the sum of its parts – an excellent sports coupé.

arrived in 1965). In Veloce spec (commonly dubbed GTV), the engine was the same mildly tuned unit as would shortly appear in the Duetto. It had bigger intake valves, higher-lift cams and a modified intake manifold. This resulted in a power boost to 110hp but more significantly torque was up from 103lb ft to 115lb ft, delivered 200rpm lower down the rev range at 2800rpm. Top speed rose to 116mph and the engine could happily rev to over 7000rpm.

Three chrome bars in the front grille and a cloverleaf badge on the C-pillars distinguished the Veloce on the outside, while very deep bucket seats greatly improved

The GTV's 1.6-litre engine was boosted to 110hp and could rev to over 7000rpm.

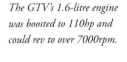

support for the front passengers. As a whole, the Veloce package worked extremely well, as *Autosport* magazine commented: "Surprisingly there is no comparison between the GT and GTV, for the very minor alterations make the Veloce a much better car... One of the most outstanding features of the Veloce is that the increase in horsepower has been obtained without a detrimental effect on flexibility." *Car* magazine added: "The GTV feels absolutely right from the moment you take the wheel... It remains a civilised machine, quiet and smooth at touring speeds... On the road, there is the immediate impression not so much of the urge as of smooth, sustained, politely controlled power that acts in concert with five perfectly chosen gear ratios and an urgent though restrained exhaust note."

The model's excellent press reception was reflected in buoyant sales figures: up to 1968, some 13,471 examples of the Giulia 1600 GTV were made.

SPECIFICATIONS	
GIULIA SPRINT GT/GTV	
Engine:	1570cc 4-cyl twin-cam
Power:	103hp @ 6000rpm/110hp @ 6000rpm
Torque:	139Nm (103lb ft) @ 3000rpm
	156Nm (115lb ft) @ 2800rpm
Transmission:	5-speed manual
Wheels:	15in steel
Weight:	1040kg/1020kg
Top speed:	111mph/116mph
0-62mph:	10.7sec/10.5sec

GIULIA 1600 GTC (1964-1966)

Arriving in 1964, the convertible GTC (the 'C' standing for 'Cabriolet') was the second model in the short-wheelbase Giulia family, although 'short' would be a more accurate description of the GTC's life cycle. The new model was the work of Carrozzeria Touring, which removed the roof, strengthened the chassis and added a convertible roof. The soft top almost completely disappeared below the waistline when stowed under its tonneau, and when the unique-to-the-GTC side windows were lowered, the car sported an exceptionally clean appearance. A removable hardtop was offered as an extra.

The GTC's four-seater cabin was almost as practical as the coupé's, as it had comparable rear headroom, although the front seats were thinner and the extra chassis bracing reduced foot room somewhat. The boot was also smaller.

Mechanically, the GTC was identical to the 1600 GT coupé, and since it weighed no more than the hardtop model, it had very similar performance figures, with only a slightly lower top speed. However, testers did note one particular issue, as *Autocar*'s road test elucidated: "The car did not

The GTC four-seater convertible was in some ways ahead of its time, but was ultimately overshadowed by the Duetto.

Elegant soft-top folded away completely out of the line of sight.

GTC's cabin echoed that of the Sprint GT but offered a proper wind-in-the-hair experience.

feel entirely rigid, and there was some scuttle shake while travelling over rough parts."

Officially launched at the 1965 Geneva Show, the 1600 GTC was destined to be a rare beast, partly because of its higher price and partly because it would soon be competing with Alfa's own Duetto Spider. Some 998 GTCs were made up until 1966, of which just 99 were right-hand drive.

The Sprint GTC badge was short-lived: less than 1000 were sold in just over a year in production.

SPECIFICATIONS	
GIULIA SPRINT GTC	
Engine:	1570cc 4-cyl twin-cam
Power:	103hp @ 6000rpm
Torque:	139Nm (103lb ft) @ 2800rpm
Transmission:	5-speed manual
Wheels:	15in steel
Weight:	1040kg
Top speed:	109mph
0-62mph:	11sec

GIULIA SPRINT GTA (1965-1975)

The Giulia TI Super saloon, with its lightened body and extra power, had performed well in motorsport (finishing fourth in the 1963 Tour de France, for instance), so it was no surprise that Alfa developed a version of the Sprint GT coupé for racing in European Touring Cars – which the model duly won in 1966, 1967 and 1968.

The road-going homologation GTA took until early 1965 to arrive (at the Amsterdam Show). This was the first Alfa Romeo ever to use the GTA badge, the "A" standing for Alleggerita (or "lightened").

And it really was lightened, the weight reduction compared to the regular Giulia Sprint totalling 220kg (the GTA tipped the scales at a mere 820kg unladen). This exceptional lightness was down to many factors, but chiefly the widespread use of aluminium for the main bodywork – which otherwise looked very like the Sprint GT's. Also shedding weight were a lack of sound insulation, no armrests, lightweight cabin parts and Plexiglas windows.

Compared to the engine in the normal Sprint GT, the GTA's 1570cc unit had a higher 9.7:1 compression ratio, larger Weber 45 carbs, uprated valves and

With its "Alleggerita" (lightened) bodywork, the GTA was intended to homologate the Sprint for competition.

In road-going form, the 1.6-litre GTA engine developed 115hp, offering great performance in this 820kg car.

The 1300 GTA Junior was homologated for low-capacity class racing.

Red-and-white paint scheme with cloverleaf and serpent decals certainly looked the part.

two spark plugs per cylinder, giving it a healthy 115hp at 6000rpm and superb tunability. For the track, it typically developed around the 170hp mark but it could go as high as 220hp in supercharged GTA-SA guise. Some mechanical components were also in lightweight alloy, including the crankcase cover and bellhousing. In a car weighing a mere 820kg, 0-60mph could be reached in 8.8 seconds, with a quarter-mile time of 16.7 seconds and top speed of 115mph.

A whole range of options was available, targeted principally at competition use, such as a limited-slip differential, wider alloy wheels, rear anti-roll bar, oil cooler, uprated exhaust, racing seats and heavy-duty clutch.

Autocar tested a rally-prepared 1600 GTA in April 1967 and said: "The grip in the wet was quite astonishing, and even on muddy patches we were able to turn on the power very early in the bends without snaking… Listening to the exhaust wailing and growling, crackling in the overrun and blasting forth with renewed strength at every gearchange, it took me back to Spa and the excitement of an endurance ordeal."

The road-spec GTA added plenty to the cost: in Italy, the price was 2,995,000 lire (compared to 2,195,000 for the regular Sprint GT), while in the UK it cost £2898 (versus £1950 for the GT). Around 500 1.6-litre GTAs were made, of which around 50 had right-hand drive.

Alfa also built a 1300 GTA Junior from June 1968, which was designed to mop up the smaller capacity racing classes. The road-going homologation Junior had a two-spark-plug-per-cylinder version of the 1290cc engine with some 96hp – fairly modest for a performance car, it must be said, but in Autodelta race spec it was capable of up to 165hp. Typically finished in red with a white stripe and cloverleaf down the side, plus a "Biscione" serpent decal on the bonnet, it cut a fine figure, even if its price was elevated: 2,198,000 lire (versus 1,695,000 for the 1300 GT Junior). The GTA Junior sold some 493 examples over a lengthy production period that stretched well into the 1970s.

At the end of the 1960s came a more potent racing model called the GTAm; some suggested the "m" stood for *maggiorata*, or "increased", referring to the adoption of an expanded 2.0-litre engine. However,

GTA Junior's power output of 96hp was quite modest but in racing spec it could go as high as 165hp.

Exclusively for racing, the GTA could be had with a 1750 engine.

Wide arches for competition accommodated bigger wheels and uprated suspension.

Alfa Romeo itself said "Am" was for "America", since this was based on the US-spec car with its Spica fuel injection system. In its ultimate spec, the 1779cc engine was bored out to 84.5mm, some 0.5mm more than the 2.0-litre unit eventually fitted to the 2000 GT Veloce in 1971 (the GTAm's engine capacity was 1985cc, the Veloce's 1962cc), and was capable of developing up to 240hp. Unlike other GTAs, the

GTAm used a steel bodyshell. Only 40 examples of the GTAm were made, all strictly for competition.

In motorsport, the GTA was frequently seen with flared arches to accommodate bigger wheels and uprated suspension. GTAs became famous for lifting a front wheel in corners – basically down to the soft rear/hard front suspension set-up – and John Bolster in *Autosport* commented that the GTA was "at its

"Cock a leg" attitude was typical of GTA's cornering, as this 1967 GTA Junior proves.

This is the Alfa Romeo Museum's very own 1750 GTAm racer.

*Advert for the Giulia 1300 Junior traded
heavily on the GTA's sporting prowess.*

best when all four wheels are sliding". The extensive
competition successes scored by GTAs in period are
beyond the scope of this book, but suffice it so say
that dozens of races, as well as a few championships,
were bagged.

A total of 1000 GTAs needed to be made for racing
homologation, which Alfa Romeo (probably) succeeded
in making over the life-cycle of the model. Today, all
GTAs are highly prized collector cars, fetching perhaps
ten times as much as a regular Giulia coupé.

1300 Junior
la Giulia che vince

La vostra GT 1300 Junior è
identica per linea,
arditezza sportiva e sicurezza
alla GTA 1300 Junior
che nel 1971 ha vinto il Cam-
pionato Europeo Turismo.
Con qualcosa in più:
la silenziosità, il conforto
e le finiture di una macchina
da grandi viaggi.

Alfa Romeo

SPECIFICATIONS

GIULIA SPRINT 1600 GTA/1300 GTA JUNIOR

Engine:	1570cc/1290cc 4-cyl twin-cam
Power:	115hp @ 6000rpm
	96hp @ 6000rpm
Torque:	142Nm (105lb ft) @ 3000rpm
	114Nm (84lb ft) @ 5600rpm
Transmission:	5-speed manual
Wheels:	14in alloy
Weight:	820kg/920kg
Top speed:	115mph/108mph
0-62mph:	9.0sec/10.0sec

While the 1300 GT Junior may not have been very fast, its sweet-revving engine was widely appreciated.

GIULIA 1300 GT JUNIOR (1966-1971)
& GIULIA 1.3 GT/1.6 GT JUNIOR (1972-1976)

A more affordable version of the Giulia GT arrived in 1966 with "Junior" badging. This used Alfa's familiar 1290cc engine, effectively the same unit as fitted to the old 101 series Giulietta Spider. With twin carbs, it produced 89hp at 5500rpm and torque of 89lb ft at 3000rpm, and was good for 108mph – not terribly fast, perhaps, but the engine was widely appreciated by road testers for its sweetness.

In 1966, Alfa Romeo launched the Giulia 1300 GT Junior with an 89hp engine and pared-down spec.

For instance, *Cars & Car Conversions* said: "There is not a lot of low-speed torque and the power starts to happen at about two-five, but with five near-perfectly spaced gear ratios at your command, who the hell cares about torque?"

You were not short-changed in terms of spec, either. The five-speed gearbox and all-round disc brakes meant it retained the sporty emphasis of the more senior model. Nor did it look that different to the 1600 GT, except for a grille with one chrome bar, plainer hubcaps and "Junior" badging. Some money was also saved by having a slightly more basic cabin.

Launched in September 1966 at Alfa Romeo's Balocco test track, the Junior quickly adopted the position of the most popular model in the coupé range. Juniors were upgraded and facelifted in line with other models in the Giulia coupé range, albeit usually slightly later than "senior" versions. For instance, the Junior didn't get the GTV's brake servo, 14-inch wheels and upgraded suspension until 1969, well over a year after the GTV.

A facelift occurred in 1971, with single headlamps rather than the 1750 GTV's twin lights, no bumper overriders and more basic interior trim. From 1972, you could also buy a GT 1600 Junior model with a 1.6-litre engine option, which filled the gap between the 1.3 and 2.0 models. The 1.6 unit was essentially a left-over from the 1960s, boasting 110hp from 1972 to 1974, and 102hp thereafter.

One final change for the GT Junior range arrived in 1974, when it received the same bodyshell as the 2000 GTV, complete with its revised rear wheelarches and double front lights, and the much plusher interior of the GTV. The 1.3-litre Junior sold 91,195 examples in all, while the 1.6-litre Junior sold 14,299, with both models lasting right up until 1976.

In 1972 came a new GT 1600 Junior version with extra power but retaining a low price tag.

Some 14,299 examples of the 1600 Junior were made – rather fewer than the 1300 Junior.

Junior models tended to be upgraded later in their life cycle than "regular" Sprint GT models.

SPECIFICATIONS

GIULIA 1300 GT JUNIOR/1600 GT JUNIOR

Engine:	1290cc/1570cc 4-cyl twin-cam
Power:	89hp @ 5500rpm
	110hp @ 6000rpm (later 102hp)
Torque:	120Nm (89lb ft) @ 3000rpm
	139Nm (103lb ft) @ 2800rpm
Transmission:	5-speed manual
Wheels:	15in or 14in steel
Weight:	990kg/1020kg
Top speed:	108mph/113mph
0-62mph:	12.6sec/10.5sec

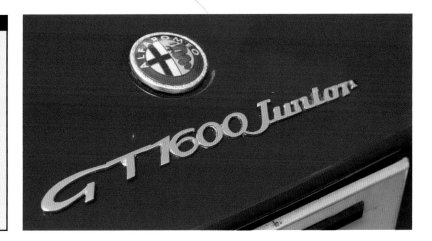

The new 1750 GT Veloce of
1967 adopted twin mythical
badges: "1750" and "Veloce".

*The new 1750 GT Veloce of
1967 adopted twin mythical
badges: "1750" and "Veloce".*

*The 1750 GTV not only had
more power but more torque,
too, making it a strong
performer.*

GIULIA 1750 GT VELOCE (1967-1973) & 2000 GT VELOCE (1971-1976)

The first major changes to Alfa's GT coupé – in fact to the whole Giulia range – arrived in 1968 when the new "1750" range was launched, whose main advance was the introduction of a new 1779cc engine. Fitted to 105 coupé, Spider and Berlina models, it was dubbed 1750 rather than 1800 to evoke Alfa's pre-war glory years. The new range debuted at the Brussels Motor Show on 17 January 1968, where it was displayed alongside a 1750 from 1932 to bring the point home.

Deserving "Veloce" status, the new (type 00548) 1779cc twin-cam engine featured a stiffer block with 2mm extra bore and 6.5mm extra stroke. The crankshaft was modified, as were the cooling and lubrication channels, while the compression ratio was raised from 9:1:1 to 9.5:1. As a result, it developed a healthy 122hp at 5000rpm but was arguably more docile than the 1600, with less need to rev it hard, partly as a result of the increase in torque, up by 19 per cent. For reasons of cleaner emissions, the American-market 1750 engine got Spica fuel injection instead of the twin Webers fitted for other markets.

Other changes introduced for the 1750 GTV included smaller-diameter but wider wheels (5.5x14 instead of 4.5x15), revised front suspension geometry, a rear anti-roll bar and upgraded brakes. A new front end was the clearest external change, with a different grille, wraparound indicators, two driving lights (in addition to headlamps) and an end to the "step front" so that the bonnet aligned cleanly with the front panel. The cabin was revised, too, notably with a fresh facia featuring two cowled dials, new three-spoke steering wheel and a different, extended centre console. Curiously, the front passenger's seat headrest was extendable, while the driver's was not.

Road testers continued to appreciate the GTV. John Bolster of *Autosport* tested the 1750 GTV in in 1968 and said: "This is a car of character and not just another automobile… [the] new model is worthy to carry those very special numerals." As for the new 1779cc engine, *Motor* magazine said: "The way it can pull from under 20mph in fifth gear with just a little throttle feeding is as impressive as it is academic for an Alfa driver… At the other end of the scale, it pulls

Smaller-diameter 14-inch wheels arguably made the GTV even better looking.

Meriting its "Veloce" status, the new 1779cc twin-cam engine developed 122hp.

smoothly and lustily all the way to the red, which starts at 6200rpm; we used 7000rpm."

1971 saw the arrival of the 2000 GT Veloce with the fitment of Alfa's new 1962cc engine, achieved by increasing the 1750's bore by 4mm (up from 80mm to 84mm). Power now rose to 132hp at 6000rpm, and a top speed of 123mph was possible; however, power would drop by 4hp to 128hp in 1975, denting performance slightly. While the 2000 Spider hardly changed in appearance, the GTV coupé received some substantial updates. Distinguishing the 2000 GTV were another restyle at the front (with the Alfa shield now standing proud of a different grille), reprofiled rear wheelarches, new wheels and wider rear light clusters incorporating reversing lights. Inside, an improved cabin featured eyeball air vents, the main instruments

Revised GTV cabin featured a new facia with twin cowled dials and an extended centre console.

(now with blue faces, curiously) were regrouped into a single cluster and the centre console now extended less far back along the transmission tunnel.

The 2000 GTV was widely praised in the press. *Autocar* called it, "a genuinely quick car with relaxed 100-110mph cruising capability" while *Car* said, "the handling is exceptionally good". But testers started to note the downsides of its ageing design: for example, the wind noise, cramped interior and awkward pedals. That was in 1971; the GTV soldiered on in production for another five years, by which time it was very long in the tooth and the Alfetta GT (see Chapter 7) had established itself as its natural successor.

Alfa's GTV models sold impressively well in period.

1750 GTV got revised front suspension, rear anti-roll bar, uprated brakes and new front end styling.

SPECIFICATIONS	
GIULIA 1750 GT VELOCE	
/2000 GT VELOCE	
Engine:	1779cc/1962cc 4-cyl twin-cam
Power:	122hp @ 5000rpm
	132hp at 6000rpm (later 128hp)
Torque:	170Nm (126lb ft) @ 2800rpm
	178Nm (132lb ft) @ 4400rpm
Transmission:	5-speed manual
Wheels:	14in steel
Weight:	1040kg
Max speed:	116mph/123mph
0-62mph:	10.4sec/9.0sec

The 2000 GTV was restyled at the front, and got reprofiled rear wheelarches and new wheels.

The 1750 GTV shifted 44,269 examples from 1967 to 1972, while the 2000 GTV sold 37,459 between 1971 and 1976. These models made a significant contribution to the total of over 225,000 examples of the Giulia Sprint/GT made during its 13-year production lifespan (a big seller in coupé terms). Today, the model retains a special aura of "Alfaness" that very few other models can match. Its shape is also highly appreciated by the design community as a classic, even if Giugiaro himself never really rated his work for Bertone.

132hp engine in the 2000 GTV gave it beefy performance.

The Giulia TZ was conceived as a lightweight coupé based on the Giulia Tipo 105 platform.

Ultra-light tubular steel chassis is clearly visible in this cutaway drawing.

GIULIA TZ (1963-1966)

The TZ was conceived by Alfa's Orazio Satta Puliga, who had full backing from Alfa Romeo to create a lightweight coupé based on his forthcoming Giulia Tipo 105. Zagato having had history with Alfa (in particular with the Giulietta SZ), the Milanese coachbuilder was top of the list to create the aluminium bodywork – and indeed, Zagato would eventually make the tubular steel chassis for the TZ, too.

However, the whole project took a very long time to get off the ground. Prototypes for a lightweight competition car based on the yet-to-be-released Tipo

105 were built as early as 1960, initially in open-top form, but distractions at Alfa Romeo – including launching the 2600 and Giulia – meant that progress stuttered. To avoid delays like these and to carry out its racing activities, Alfa decided to set up a separate competitions department, not only for the TZ but for several other projects, too. The man tasked with directing the new operation was Carlo Chiti, the engineer whose work at Ferrari was so highly lauded. He made a new life for himself after his Cavallino Rampante career with Alfa Romeo's competition department, Autodelta (initially Auto-Delta), an

enterprise formed in association with an Innocenti dealer called Ludovico Chizzola of Udine, near Venice. Autodelta would assemble the new TZ, the letters standing for Tubolare Zagato, after the model's tubular chassis and the Zagato-developed design.

The tubular steel chassis, designed by Edo Mazoni, weighed a mere 40kg yet was immensely strong. The rear suspension was independent by wishbones and upper radius arms – Alfa's first post-war IRS. Inboard rear disc brakes helped reduce unsprung weight, and overall the TZ tipped the scales at a mere 660kg. Ercole Spada's design was also notably aerodynamic, with a distinctive Kamm tail and quirky "trefoil" profile.

Alfa's 1570cc engine had the same level of tune as the Giulia SS (112hp) but when tuned by Conrero it could reach as much as 170hp. In road tune, the TZ could attain 134mph, which was an excellent figure for the power output.

Road & Track magazine described the TZ as: "A proper bit of customers' racing machinery… Those of you who want to have bags of fun and race successfully couldn't do much better."

The first production cars were completed in the latter half of 1963 and called Giulia TZ (alternatively GTZ and, in retrospect, TZ1). 100 examples needed to be built to homologate it for GT racing, and this was achieved, just: some 112 TZs were made by Autodelta in all. In racing, the TZ scored many successes in prestigious events such as Le Mans, Nürburgring and Targa Florio.

S P E C I F I C A T I O N S	
GIULIA TZ	
Engine:	1570cc 4-cyl twin-cam
Power:	112hp @ 6500rpm
Torque:	131Nm (97lb ft) @ 4200rpm
Transmission:	5-speed manual
Wheels:	15in steel
Weight:	660kg
Top speed:	134mph
0-62mph:	N/A

TZ stood for Tubolare Zagato, after the car's tubular chassis and Zagato design. Weighing just 660kg, the TZ performed superbly considering its modest power output.

The TZ's 112hp 1570cc engine was shared with the Giulia SS but could be tuned by Conrero as high as 170hp.

The Giulia TZ enjoyed a successful Autodelta-backed racing career. Here, two TZs tussle at the 1965 Le Mans.

GIULIA TZ2 (1965-1967)

By 1965, the TZ had lost its competitive edge in racing, so Autodelta developed a substantially revised version, the TZ2. Having experimented with glassfibre bodies for the TZ, and finding that some 30kg could be shaved off the weight of the car, it was decided to make the new model's body from plastic. The all-new bodywork featured a single Plexiglas rear window instead of the TZ's three-window set-up and had a notably low roof line, giving a semi-reclining driving position. The TZ2 was not only lighter – weighing a mere 620kg in dry form – but more aerodynamic, too.

The 1.6-litre engine gained an eight-plug cylinder head, similar to the GTA's, and thus developed 170hp

The TZ2 enjoys an almost mythical status. Only nine chassis were made, and no two examples were exactly alike.

Forward-hinging bonnet revealed GTA-style eight-plug 1.6-litre engine with 170hp.

at 7500rpm. It was also dry-sumped, permitting a lower bonnet line, while the suspension and steering were revised and the whole car sat lower down, with larger magnesium wheels providing more grip.

The TZ2's story is a little murky; indeed, it's often seen as a somewhat mythical creature with its own folkloric set of suppositions. However it's thought that nine TZ2 chassis were made in all. Class wins were scored by the TZ2 in the Targa Florio and at Sebring in 1965 and 1966, but Alfa Romeo's works racing programme soon switched to the Tipo 33 and Giulia GTA.

Unique glassfibre bodywork featured a Plexiglas rear window. The TZ2 weighed just 620kg.

The TZ-based Bertone Canguro was designed by Giugiaro and could have made production, but didn't.

Another TZ-chassised concept car was Pininfarina's swoopy Giulia Sport of 1965.

The wild OSI Scarabeo used a mid-mounted Giulia GTA 115hp engine, but sadly production plans came to naught.

STILLBORN ODDITIES

Both Bertone and Pininfarina made one-off show cars based on the TZ chassis, the former with the Canguro, the latter with the Giulia Sport. The Canguro appeared on Bertone's stand at the 1964 Paris Show featuring a Giugiaro-penned shape that was much more harmonious than the TZ's, including cut-in curved windows and a superbly elegant rear end. There were reportedly plans to do a limited production run but Alfa Romeo, in its wisdom, declined.

A few months later, at the 1965 Turin Show, Pininfarina showed its TZ2-based Giulia Sport. Designed by Aldo Brovarone, its distinctively curved shape owed a lot to the same man's Ferrari Dino concept of the same year. Considering the fact that Ferrari leapt on the Dino idea, it's small wonder that no production run awaited Pininfarina's Alfa.

One further coupé, the OSI Scarabeo, came closer to having a production life as an official Alfa Romeo. A prototype H-shaped chassis was designed and sent to the Turin-based coachbuilder, OSI. Presented in 1966, this was a quite radical design. The very low (102cm high) wedge-shaped body featured a centre section that lifted up for access to the two seats. It used a 1570cc Giulia GTA 115hp engine mounted transversely behind the seats. Three prototypes were built, all with somewhat differing bodies, including one open-top Spider. There was a plan to make 500 cars to homologate it for racing but Alfa Romeo had other irons in the fire, ultimately resulting in the mid-engined Alfa Romeo 33 racer taking the Scarabeo's place; OSI's project was summarily canned.

Neo-classic novelty: the Giulia 1600 Zagato Gran Sport 4R evoked Alfa's pre-war 6C 1750.

GIULIA 1600 ZAGATO GRAN SPORT 4R (1966-1968)

"Replicars" or "neo-classics" have become a familiar sub-branch of the motoring world in recent times, but in 1966 the idea was very fresh. The story of Alfa Romeo's very own neo-classic is a curious one; in fact, it was perhaps the first throwback model made in Europe (the idea having originated in the late 1950s in the USA).

The brainchild of Gianni Mazzocchi, the publisher of Italy's leading motoring magazine, *Quattroruote*, the idea was to match pre-war Alfa 6C 1750 styling with modern running gear. For the design work, Ercole Spada of Zagato was approached. He used Mazzocchi's own personal 1930 6C 1750 roadster as a template – somewhat ironically, as it was a Touring-bodied example, not a Zagato.

Underneath sat an Alfa Romeo Giulia TI saloon floorpan with hand-beaten vintage-style body panels welded on top. Braking was by drums, sited behind 15-inch Borrani wire wheels (which really looked too small for a vintage car). The detailing was impeccable, though, including a nickel-plated fold-down windscreen.

The prototype was first seen in April 1965, with production starting a year later at Zagato's factory. Remarkably, the car was sold as an official Alfa Romeo model through dealerships in Italy, called the Gran Sport 4R (the 4R indicating Quattroruote magazine). Priced at 2,360,000 lire, it was hardly cheap, and while it was lightweight, its inferior aerodynamics meant it was far slower than regular Giulias; indeed, it only managed 92mph and 0-60mph in 12 seconds when *Motor* magazine tested it. Only 82 examples were ever made.

S P E C I F I C A T I O N S	
GIULIA 1600 ZAGATO GRAN SPORT 4R	
Engine:	1570cc four-cyl twin-cam
Power:	90hp @ 6000rpm
Torque:	119Nm (88lb ft) @ 4400rpm
Transmission:	5-speed manual
Wheels:	15in wire
Weight:	750kg
Top speed:	92mph
0-62mph:	12sec

The Zagato Gran Sport 4R project was initiated by the Italian car magazine, Quattroruote.

Unusual in most respects, the Giulia 1300 GT Junior Z had a unique stylistic character.

GIULIA 1300 GT JUNIOR Z (1969-1972) & GIULIA 1600 GT JUNIOR Z (1972-1975)

By rights, Zagato's Junior Z should have been an absolute hit: here was a focused, two-seater coupé that inherited some of the glory of Zagato's Alfa SZ and TZ. But in reality, its "Junior" designation and the fact that it never really enjoyed a life in competitive motorsport meant that it was destined to remain a quirky sidebar in Alfa's coupé story.

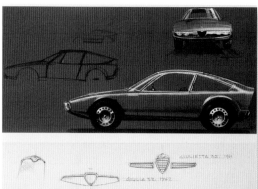

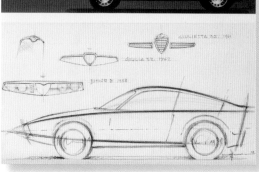

Ercole Spada of Zagato was responsible for the Giulia Junior Z's design, as evidenced by his sketches shown here.

While Zagato's bodywork was aerodynamic, the fact that it was made from steel meant it was only marginally lighter than the Bertone-bodied Giulia 1300 Junior (weighing 950kg). Its eccentric styling and high list price – this was the third most expensive Alfa in the range behind the Montreal and 1300 GTA – did it few favours, either.

Launched at the 1969 Turin Salon, the Junior Z certainly widened the appeal of Alfa's 1300 Junior range by adding a strict two-seater model. It was styled by Zagato's chief designer, Ercole Spada, who added such unusual features as a Plexiglas nose and a sharply cut-off Kamm tail.

In contrast to the Bertone-styled Giulia coupés, the Junior Z's cabin was much more driver-focused, with a leatherette-trimmed dash, gear lever emerging almost horizontally from the centre console and low-set bucket seats with built-in headrests. Luggage was loaded in via a rear hatch, which also served another curious function: it could be raised up very slightly at the press of a button to enable stale cabin air to be extracted more easily.

The mechanical basis was the Alfa Spider, whose floorpan was shortened behind the rear wheels, on to which Zagato then added new inner panels and the main bodywork in steel (although the bonnet and doors were aluminium). In a highly contorted production process that was every bit as quirky as the

The shape may have been aerodynamic, but this wasn't a particularly light car at 950kg.

Rear view of this 1600 Junior Z shows the idiosyncratic hatchback, which could be opened for ventilation.

The cabin was also unique to the Junior Z, with a leatherette-trimmed dash and the gear lever sprouting quirkily from the centre console.

car itself, the Junior Z was assembled by Maggiora of Turin, then sent to Alfa for priming, then to Zagato for painting and trimming and finally back to Alfa for engines to be fitted.

The 89hp 1290cc twin-cam was used initially, good enough for 108mph. In November 1972, it was replaced by the 1600 Junior Zagato (actually badged 1600 Z). While the 1300 Junior Z had a 105 chassis prefix, the new 1600 Z was a Tipo 115 (115.24). With its more powerful 110hp 1.6-litre engine, the top speed rose to 118mph. These later Zs had a slightly longer tail, 2000 Berlina tail-lights, a fuel tank borrowed from the Spider and pendant foot pedals. A total of 1108 examples of the 1300 version were made, plus 402 examples of the 1600 up to 1975, making 1510 Junior Zs in all.

SPECIFICATIONS	
GIULIA 1300/1600 GT JUNIOR Z	
Engine:	11290cc/1570cc 4-cyl
	twin-cam
Power	89hp @ 5500rpm
	110bp @ 6000rpm
Torque	120Nm (89lb ft) @ 3000rpm
	139Nm (103lb ft) @ 2800rpm
Transmission	5-speed manual
Wheels	14in steel
Weight	950kg
Max speed	108mph/118mph
0-62mph	11.8sec/9.3sec

An odd Plexiglas panel covered the lights, into which was inserted an Alfa Romeo grille (of sorts).

DUETTO
& SPIDER

SPIDER 1600 DUETTO (1966-1968)

The replacement for the 101 series Giulia Spider was the Duetto, launched at the Geneva Motor Show on 10 March 1966. In fact, it originally had no name. Instead, the public was invited to enter a competition to suggest a name. Of the 140,501 entries received, "Duetto" was chosen as the winner, and a man called Guidobaldi Trionfi from Brescia received one of the brand new cars as a prize for suggesting it.

The origins of Pininfarina's smooth, rounded profile and scalloped sides can be traced right back to the design house's Super Flow concept of 1956, while the transparent headlamp cowls were previewed in Farina's 1957 Super Flow 2. The 105 Spider's direct forerunner, however, was a 1961 Turin Show prototype called the Giulietta Spider Speciale Aerodinamica, which used Giulietta mechanicals and bore clear hallmarks of the eventual production shape.

This was the very last design that Pininfarina created under Battista "Pinin" Farina's watch. He lived just long enough to see the new car enter production, since he passed away in April 1966, barely one month after the presentation of the Duetto.

The bodywork was low and artfully sculpted, incorporating a degree of curvature below the waistline that was startling, even for 1966. Much was done to keep the shape as clean as possible, with a low-set front end, integrated bumpers and grille, Perspex headlamp cowls and a soft-top that folded almost completely out of sight. The car's excellent aerodynamics were confirmed by Pininfarina's wind tunnel testing at Turin Polytechnic (although no Cd figure was ever released). Less certain was the effectiveness of the body side "scallops", which were claimed to enhance directional stability in side winds.

The traditional Alfa shield grille was incorporated very low down, with a circular Alfa Romeo badge protruding slightly above the nose line, while the bonnet hinged at its forward edge. Badging on the Duetto was notable by its absence. Alfa Romeo never even created a badge reading "Duetto"; instead it was referred to in most promotional literature as the Spider 1600, perhaps because a confectionery manufacturer

Alfa Romeo's Duetto was a highly curvaceous, low-slung sports car.

Pininfarina's Giulietta Spider Speciale Aerodinamica of 1961 gave clear indications as to how the later Duetto would look.

The distinctive rounded tail gave rise to this car's nickname, "osso di sepia", or "cuttlefish".

already had a product called Duetto.

The round-tail shape was known in Italy as osso di seppia or cuttlefish, for obvious reasons. It was quite controversial at the time, viewed as contrived and fussy in its details. In its road test, *Road & Track* magazine said sniffily: "No-one of the staff was wild about the car's shape." George Bishop of *Car* magazine described it as the "ugly sister" of the prettier Bertone GT. But as the years have rolled by, the *coda lunga* (long-tail, or round-tail) shape has acquired a status as the most favoured Spider body style of all.

The interior was either tastefully simple or Spartan, depending on your viewpoint. For instance, the dashboard was painted the same colour as the bodywork, and you had rubber floor mats instead of carpets. The seat design was more effective than that in other 105 models, while behind the seats lay a vinyl-lined area that could perhaps fit two very small children, but more likely luggage. The folding soft-top's ease of operation earned it praise from

The Duetto shared its 110hp, 1.6-litre engine with the Giulia GTV, as well as its five-speed gearbox.

Fabulously period image of the Alfa Spider as launched in 1966.

many quarters – indeed, it is still regarded as one of the best ever in an open-topped two-seater – while a Pininfarina-designed hardtop was an optional extra.

In construction, the Duetto was an all-steel welded monocoque with triple sills for strength. At 2250mm, the wheelbase was identical to the old 101 Spider's, but 260mm shorter than the Giulia saloon's, and 100mm shorter than the Giulia Sprint's. Pininfarina built the bodies at its Grugliasco plant in the suburbs of Turin, then transported them by road to Alfa's Arese factory in Milan, where the mechanicals and trim were installed.

A beautifully simple dashboard lent an air of purity to the Italian sports car ideal that the Duetto represented.

Guidobaldi Trionfi, the winner of a contest to name the Duetto, receives the keys to a new car as his prize.

With optional hardtop in place, the Duetto became an all-season prospect.

The Duetto shared its 110hp, 1.6-litre engine with the Giulia GTV, as well as the five-speed gearbox, although the gear lever was set at more of an angle because the driver sat further back compared to other 105 series models. Performance was sprightly, if not class-leading: a top speed of 113mph and 0-62mph in 11 seconds.

Road testers heaped praise on how well the Duetto drove. "The overall impression is one of great responsiveness," said *Road & Track* magazine, "and the feeling that the car is an extension of the driver at the controls is unmistakably clear. The steering is excellent – light, accurate and among the best we've ever encountered in any car... The Duetto sits much flatter in the turns than the Giulia."

Meanwhile *Motor* magazine said: "It pulls well from surprisingly low speeds and has commendable smoothness right to the tachometer limit of 6200rpm... It seems natural to use all these revs

whenever the opportunity arises."

When it was launched in March 1966 the list price was 2,195,000 lire, which was a touch expensive (Fiat's 1600S Cabriolet cost 1,800,000 lire at the time). In Britain the Duetto was priced at almost £1900, against £1553 for the Lotus Elan and £1967 for Jaguar's E-Type, both of which regularly bettered the Alfa in contemporary group road tests. In America it was more of a level playing field: the Duetto cost $3950, cheaper than the Elan's $4545 price tag. America would quickly become the Spider's most important market.

The model received a huge boost in profile when Dustin Hoffman drove one in the 1967 film, *The Graduate*. Although sales of the model started slowly – it was substantially slower-selling than the old Giulietta Spider – they definitely picked up as time progressed, in the USA especially. Some 6335 Duettos were made between 1966 and 1968, of which 382 were right-hand drive.

SPECIFICATIONS	
SPIDER 1600 DUETTO	
Engine:	1570cc 4-cyl twin-cam
Power:	110hp @ 6000rpm
Torque:	139Nm (103lb ft) @ 2800rpm
Transmission:	5-speed manual
Wheels:	15in steel
Weight:	990kg
Max speed:	113mph
0-62mph:	11.0sec

*Changes for the 1750 Spider
included revised suspension,
larger brakes and smaller
14-inch wheels.*

SPIDER 1750 VELOCE (1967-1969)
& SPIDER 1300 JUNIOR (1968-1969)

It had been intended to replace the 1600 Duetto at a
single stroke in January 1968 with a two-model range
– the 1300 Junior and the 1750 Spider Veloce – but
a delay in the launch of the 1300 (it finally arrived in
June 1968) meant that the 1600 Duetto was offered
alongside the 1750 Spider Veloce for a time as the
"entry-level" Spider at a reduced price.

The Duetto name was now dropped in favour of
"1750 Spider Veloce" badging. The 1779cc engine
was taken straight from the 1750 Berlina, with 122hp
(unless you were an American buyer, that is, in which

*In 1967, the Duetto name
was dropped as the new 1750
Spider Veloce received a larger
engine.*

*The slightly cheaper 1300
Junior of 1968 could be
identified by its more basic
trim and lack of headlamp
fairings.*

A major evolution occurred in 1969, when the old round tail gave way to a cut-off Series 2 Kamm rear end.

case fuel injection dropped the power to 115hp). The 1750's final drive ratio was now higher than before, so that cruising was more relaxed, and a ZF limited slip differential was offered as an optional extra. To match the extra power and speed, a new transverse anti-roll bar at the rear was added to the front one. There were softer springs all round and the front end geometry was altered to curtail body roll. The rear brake discs were also larger, and in place of 15-inch wheels were new 14-inch rims with wider 165 tyres to improve grip and ride quality.

The Spider's sharper handling was recognised in press reports. *Road & Track* magazine commented: "The rear anti-roll bar… reduced the traditional Alfa Romeo understeer… As speeds increase there is a gradual transition from understeer to oversteer…. The

car can be cornered cleanly by anyone; those skilful enough to deserve a car like this can vary the attitude with more power. Stability for the prudent, sport for the enthusiastic."

As for the 1300 Junior of 1968, mechanically it mirrored the GT Junior coupé; it differed from the 1750 in having more basic trim and lacking headlamp fairings. A total of 5497 examples of the round-tail 1750 Spider Veloce were made up until 1969, of which 494 were RHD. A further 2880 examples of the 1300 Spider Junior were made, 180 of them RHD.

SPIDER SERIES 2 1750 VELOCE (1969-1972) & 1300 JUNIOR (1969-1977)

The biggest single change in the lifespan of the Spider came at the Turin Motor Show on 29 October 1969, when the round tail was replaced by a cut-off Kamm rear end (in Italy, called coda tronca or short-tail). This model is often referred to as the Series 2.

The restyling work was done by Pininfarina, with much testing carried out in the wind tunnel, resulting in strident claims about aerodynamic enhancement. The boot lid profile was near-horizontal and the tail ended in a sharp, vertical chop. The shape and construction of the rear wings also changed, as did the rear lighting with its rectangular clusters incorporating reversing lamps. The tail chop reduced the car's overall length by 130mm (from 4250mm to 4120mm). Apparently defying logic, the shortened tail actually produced a more generous overall luggage

SPECIFICATIONS	
SPIDER 1750 VELOCE/1300 JUNIOR	
Engine:	1779cc/1290cc 4-cyl twin-cam
Power:	122hp @ 5000rpm/89hp @ 5500rpm
Torque:	170Nm (126lb ft) @ 2800rpm
	120Nm (89lb ft) @ 3000rpm
Transmission:	5-speed manual
Wheels:	14in steel
Weight:	1040kg/990kg
Max speed:	117mph/104mph
0-62mph:	9.5sec/12.5sec

Subtle Series 2 changes included all-new glass, a redesigned soft-top, and new lighting and bumpers.

The 1300 Junior also progressed to Series 2 guise, again with more basic trim.

volume, from 210 litres up to 300 litres, because the boot was deeper.

Other subtler changes included all-new glass, a redesigned soft-top, revised lighting, new bumpers and a wider, squatter Alfa front grille. In the cabin, changes moved the Spider from the 1960s and into the 1970s with a moulded plastic dashboard, recessed instruments and a centre console with rocker switches. However, in typically quirky Alfa style, the Junior retained the old-style interior.

Some changes were made to the 1779cc engine to coincide with the Kamm-tail revamp, consisting of new pistons and liners and a lower compression ratio that dropped power to 118hp (4hp down on before). Left-hand drive cars switched to pendant-type brake and clutch pedals, adopted in conjunction with new dual-circuit braking (right-hand drive cars stuck with old-style floor-hinged pedals).

Whatever the aerodynamic merits or otherwise of the new shape, it was well received by the press and public. The 1750 Spider Veloce only lasted until June 1971, when it was replaced by the larger-engined 2000 Veloce. The 1300 Junior model was also given the Kamm-tail treatment, and when the 2000 Spider

Veloce replaced the 1750 in 1971, Alfa Romeo took the opportunity to add an extra 1600 Junior model to the range in addition (see below); the 1300 Junior continued in production until 1977.

The total number of Spider Veloce 1750 models produced from 1967 to 1973 was 4674, plus a further 4027 USA 1750 Spider Veloces produced 1968-1972. As for the 1300 Junior, some 7237 examples were produced from 1968 to 1978.

S P E C I F I C A T I O N S	
SPIDER 1750 VELOCE/1300 JUNIOR	
Engine:	1779cc/1290cc 4-cyl twin-cam
Power	118hp @ 5000rpm
	89hp @ 5500rpm
Torque	170Nm (126lb ft) @ 2800rpm
	120Nm (89lb ft) @ 3000rpm
Transmission	5-speed manual
Wheels	14in steel
Weight	1040kg/1020kg
Max speed	117mph/104mph
0-62mph	9.5sec/12.5sec

A new 2000 Spider Veloce arrived in 1971, its 1962cc engine boasting 132hp.

The 2.0-litre Spider sold very healthily in the 1970s, particularly in the USA.

SPIDER SERIES 2 2000 VELOCE (1971-1982) & 1600 JUNIOR/VELOCE (1972-1981)

The new 2000 Spider Veloce was launched on 21 June 1971, alongside the rest of Alfa's new 2000 range. The only significant alteration over the Kamm-tail 1750 was the bigger engine, with a 4mm wider bore taking capacity up to 1962cc. The power output grew from 118hp to 132hp at 6000rpm, and while peak torque rose modestly from 126lb ft to 134lb ft at 3500rpm, the chief benefit was that the whole torque curve was flatter. Performance figures were better: for instance, *Autocar* magazine recorded a 0-60mph time of 8.8 seconds. The only distinguishing external features of

the new car were "2000" badging and new hub caps.

To drive, the new 2000 was improved in many ways. The engine's flatter torque curve made driving far more relaxed, and pulling away from low revs was much easier. Gear changes were also required less frequently and the higher overall power made it a quicker car. As *Sports Car World* in Australia put it, it felt a more "masculine" engine: "The engines are torquier from lower revs, feel more full-bellied – and this impression tends to filter right through the car." However, the 2.0-litre unit did not rev as high or as willingly as the 1750, and lost some of the twin-cam's familiar sweetness, as SCW explained: "It doesn't appear to have quite

New hub caps were a minor distinguishing feature of the 2000, which offered a more relaxed drive.

the sparkle of the little [1750] engine above 4000rpm… For this reason it could perhaps be described as less of an endearing enthusiasts' engine… But for everyday use the 2000 is preferable."

The 2000 Spider Veloce kicked off a long career during which it sold extremely healthily. In April 1972, Alfa Romeo added an extra model to the range, filling the gap between the 1300 Junior and 2000 Veloce: this was the 1600 Spider Junior. The old 1.6 engine, last seen in the Duetto four years previously, was fitted as part of a rationalisation process that was thought far reaching enough for a new chassis prefix – '115' – to be adopted.

1974 saw a detuning of the 1600 powerplant (102hp rather than 110hp), a similar fate also awaiting the 2000 model the following year (dropping to 128hp at 5300rpm). Smart looking Turbina magnesium alloy wheels also became an option in 1974 (standard in the USA), echoing the look of the Alfa Romeo Montreal's wheels.

Right-hand drive Spider production ended in Italy in 1977, forcing Alfa Romeo GB to cease selling the Spider in 1978, although independent specialists continued to import LHD cars, sometimes with right-hand drive conversions. South Africa also made around 300 RHD Spiders between 1975 and 1978.

In 1979 came a revamp in the cabin, including full carpeting, better safety features, new door trims, repositioned switchgear and the option of leather upholstery. In 1980, the 1600 was uprated to Veloce specification as part of a Spider "unification" process, but the 1600 was finally withdrawn from European markets in 1981.

US cars continued to have fuel injection, then from 1978 a catalytic converter and, from 1979, variable valve timing. American Spiders increasingly diverged from European ones – for instance, from 1975 they suffered from 5mph impact bumpers, while there were also special dress-up models like the 1978 Niki Lauda edition. In 1982, American Spiders finally ditched the troublesome Spica fuel injection in favour of more reliable Bosch L-Jetronic electronic injection, for which enthusiasts breathed a sigh of relief.

Alfa Romeo's figures put production of the 2.0-litre Spider in 132hp form (1971-1977) at 7368, plus a further 8952 with the 128hp engine (1975-1982), plus 22,059 Spiders for the USA (1971-1982). That's a grand total of 38,379 Spider 2000s. As for the Spider 1600, some 2371 were made with the 110hp engine (1972-1975), plus a further 2477 with 102hp (1974-1981), making a total of 4848.

S P E C I F I C A T I O N S	
SPIDER 2000 VELOCE/1600 JUNIOR	
Engine:	1962cc/1570cc 4-cyl twin-cam
Power:	132hp @ 5500rpm (later 128hp)
	110hp @ 6000rpm (later 102hp)
Torque:	182Nm (134lb ft) @ 3500rpm
	(later 180Nm/132lb ft)
	140Nm (103lb ft) @ 2800rpm
	(later 142Nm/105lb ft)
Transmission:	5-speed manual
Wheels:	14in or 15in steel or alloy
Weight:	1040kg (US: 1107kg)/1020kg
Max speed:	118mph/115mph
0-62mph:	9.0sec/11.0sec

The S3 Spider arrived in 1983 sporting wraparound bumpers and tweaks which earned it the name "Spider Aerodinamica".

SPIDER SERIES 3 1.6/2.0 & QV (1983-1989)

The third series Spider arrived at the 1983 Geneva Motor Show, marking the first major Spider overhaul since the switch from round-tail to Kamm tail in 1969. New wraparound bumpers and front and rear spoilers – the rear one made of deformable rubberised material – were the most obvious cosmetic changes, inspiring this model's common name of "Spider Aerodinamica", although it is also widely referred to as the Series 3. The new bumpers added 150mm to the car's overall length, the headlamp covers disappeared and there was a move towards matt black for external detailing and interior trim, while the front "grille" was effectively reduced to a mere bumper ornament.

In most European markets, two Spider models were offered: 1.6 (104hp) and 2.0 (128hp), which were virtually identical except for engine capacity. In America, only the 2.0 model was offered, called the 2000 Spider Veloce, although a stripped-out "Graduate" version joined it in 1985, recalling the Spider's most celebrated film role as the fated transport of Dustin Hoffman in the classic Hollywood film, *The Graduate*.

At the 1986 Geneva Show, a mid-life revision

Two engines were offered in the S3: 128hp 2.0 (pictured here) and 104hp 1.6.

As part of a 1986 mid-life range review, a new top-spec Quadrifoglio Verde model was added.

occurred. All models received a new interior featuring a single instrument housing, new fresh air vents, padded under-dash rail, and different console, seats and door trim. The big news was the launch of a range-topping Quadrifoglio Verde model (called simply Quadrifoglio in the USA), so named because of the four-leaf clover design, as immortalised by Alfa's early racing cars. The QV had a full body styling kit, wide alloy wheels, leather upholstery and a hardtop. However, not everyone was a fan of the QV's over-wrought style, it must be said.

In 1988, production transferred from Alfa's Arese factory to Pininfarina's works in Turin, where the 100,000th Spider emerged from the factory the same year. The Series 3 Aerodinamica Spider remained in production until 1989. Some 31,808 examples of the S3 2.0 were made, plus a further 4553 examples of the 1.6.

Controversial spoilers were part of the S3 package, the rear one made of deformable rubberised material.

The Spider 1.6 was sold mostly in continental Europe.

S P E C I F I C A T I O N S

SPIDER S3 1.6/2.0

Engine:	1570cc/1962cc 4-cyl twin-cam
Power:	104hp @ 5500rpm
	128hp @ 5300rpm
Torque:	137Nm (101lb ft) @ 4300rpm
	180Nm (132lb ft) @ 4300rpm
Transmission:	5-speed manual
Wheels:	14in steel or alloy
Weight:	1020kg/1040kg (US: 1155kg)
Max speed:	112mph/115mph
0-62mph:	11.0sec/9.0sec

Alfa's Series 4 Spider of 1990 was a successful stylistic update effected by Pininfarina.

SPIDER SERIES 4 1.6/2.0 (1990-1994)

In contrast to the piecemeal evolution of the Spider thus far, the Series 4 of 1990 represented a decisive and major upgrade. Sergio Pininfarina and Renzo Carli oversaw a restyle that was universally acclaimed, marking a return to clean, simple lines. Its all-new nose recalled the original Duetto's, while a longer tail mellowed the profile of the rear end, emphasised by a full-width strip of red across the back.

The S4 was less revolutionary in terms of the

The 2.0 engine gained Bosch electronic fuel injection and ignition, with variable valve timing now standard.

The S4's longer tail was filled with a strip of red across the back.

The S4 looked best of all the generations with a hardtop fitted.

A taste of the colourful Series 4 range offered from 1990 to 1994.

cockpit and mechanicals, though: here, the age-old formula was merely tweaked. One significant advance was the arrival of ZF power steering for 2.0-litre Spiders. There remained a 1.6-litre model for certain European countries (keeping non-assisted steering) but by far the more popular engine was the 2.0-litre.

While the 1.6 stuck with twin carbs, the 2.0 engine was given Bosch Motronic electronic fuel injection and ignition, with variable valve timing now standard. Unfortunately, power and torque went down as a result (to 126hp at 5800rpm), so performance was not as lusty as previous 2.0-litre Spiders. Non-catalysed

Cutaway illustration shows the essentially unchanged nature of the final Spider, almost 30 years on.

engines were sold in most EU countries until new emissions laws in 1993 forced all engines to become catalyst-equipped, in which case power dropped to 120hp. The Series 4 also marked the Spider's return to the UK market after an absence of 13 years, albeit only in left-hand drive (although an approved right-hand drive conversion was also offered).

Some 75 per cent of Series 4 production was destined for the USA, so it was fitting that the very last Commemorative Edition cars were sold exclusively in the USA in 1994. Another US peculiarity was the option of a three-speed automatic transmission; the first and only time the 105/115 Alfa Spider ever had this.

All Series 4s were built by Pininfarina, the last ones apparently made in 1993, with sales continuing into 1994 in many markets. Some 18,456 units of the Series 4 2.0 were made, plus 2951 1.6s. The grand old Spider was finally replaced in 1994 by a very different, all-new Spider: the front-wheel drive Tipo 916. The grand total of Spiders built from 1966 to 1994 was 124,104.

SPECIFICATIONS	
SPIDER S4 1.6/2.0	
Engine:	1570cc/1962cc 4-cyl twin-cam
Power:	109hp @ 6000rpm
	126hp @ 5800rpm
	(120hp with catalyst)
Torque:	137Nm (101lb ft) @ 4800rpm
	168Nm (124lb ft) @ 4200rpm
	(157Nm/116lb ft with catalyst)
Transmission	5-speed manual
	(2.0: 3-speed auto option)
Wheels	14in or 15in steel or alloy
Weight	1070kg/1110kg (US: 1156kg)
Max speed	112mph/118mph
0-62mph	10.0sec/9.0sec

The Series 4 cabin was not a huge advance on earlier Spiders; indeed it remained resolutely classic in feel.

Chapter Six

33 & MONTREAL:

ALFA'S V8s

Alfa Romeo's history of eight-cylinder cars is both long and illustrious, starting with the P2 Gran Premio of 1924, through the Tipo B (or P3) of 1932, the glorious 8C models of the 1930s, and on to the Grand Prix-winning Tipo 158 and 159 Alfetta racers of the immediate post-war years.

However, eight-cylinder engines disappeared from Alfa's world for 14 years, from 1951 until 1966. At that point, Carlo Chiti of Autodelta boldly reintroduced eight-cylinder power at Alfa Romeo. He had

designed a racing 1995cc V8 that shared much with the ATS Formula 1 engine from several years before; this V8 would effectively be his "dowry" to Alfa Romeo when it subsumed Autodelta in 1966. The V8 had Lucas indirect ignition and pumped out an impressive 270hp in race spec. Placed in the Alfa 33/2 racer, it won many significant events, including the Targa Florio, 1000km of Nürburgring, 24 Hours of Le Mans, Mugello and Imola.

Remarkably, Alfa Romeo made a road-going version

Alfa Romeo's first-ever V8 engine was engineered by Carlo Chiti of Autodelta, and fitted to the 33.

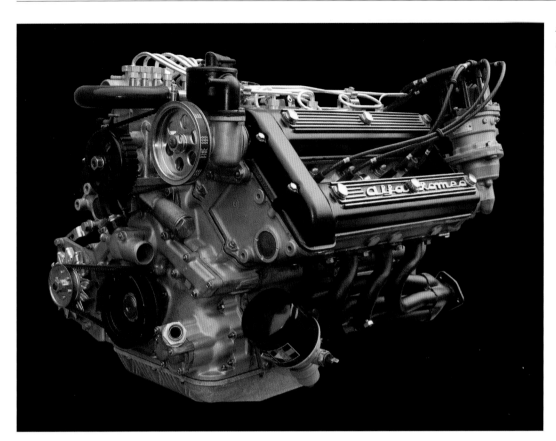

As adapted to the fit the Alfa Romeo Montreal, the V8 was expanded from 2.0 litres to 2.6.

of its 33 racer, which was called the 33 Stradale. This was Alfa's first post-war road-going eight-cylinder car when it was launched in 1967. The very definition of exotic, it was a racer in sublimely beautiful clothing, but always an extremely specialised machine.

A more commercial home for Chiti's V8 was found soon after, being adapted to power the spectacular Montreal in 1970. In expanded 2.6-litre but detuned 200hp guise, the V8 was adapted to its new role as a grand tourer. Gandini's dramatic styling – even after the compromises that beset his original shape – was, and remains, one of the biggest draws for this exceptional car. The Montreal was always a rare and exotic animal, though, and fewer than 4000 examples were built up to 1977. Alfa's first V8 era came to an end, and wouldn't be revived until the company collaborated with Maserati on the 8C Competizione some three decades later.

33 STRADALE (1967-1969)

When, in 1967, Alfa Romeo decided to clothe the mechanicals of its racing 33/2 (the figure 2 indicating the 2.0-litre displacement) with a refined road car (Stradale) body, it turned to Franco Scaglione, who more than a decade earlier had created the extraordinary Alfa Romeo BAT concepts.

Giuseppe Busso and Orazio Satta Puliga's tubular steel racing chassis was extended by 100mm in the wheelbase to make the 33 Stradale. To strengthen it, the central chassis was fabricated in sheet steel and the subframes were largely made of magnesium. Scaglione's design was surely one of the most stunningly beautiful cars ever made, and ultra-low at just 990mm tall. Since the body was made of plastic, weight was kept extremely low (just 700kg). One highly unusual feature was hinging the doors from the top of the windscreen, creating the "scissor" door that would become Lamborghini's signature in the following decade.

SPECIFICATIONS	
33 STRADALE	
Engine:	1995cc V8 twin-cam
Power:	230hp at 8800rpm
Torque:	206Nm (152lb ft) @ 7000rpm
Transmission:	6-speed manual
Wheels:	13in alloy
Weight:	700kg
Max speed:	161mph
0-62mph:	5.6sec

The Tipo 33 Stradale was an extraordinary project on just about every level. Franco Scaglione's design was extremely low and notably aerodynamic.

This was an utterly exotic machine, essentially a racer with the bare minimum of refinements, since Alfa's stated brief was to deliver 95% of the racing 33's performance. Suspension was independent all round by wishbones, coil springs and hydraulic dampers, with anti-roll bars both front and rear, while the brakes were vented discs on all four corners.

As adapted for road use, the 90-degree V8 used Spica mechanical injection, dry-sump lubrication, four coils, two plugs per cylinder and twin distributors. Offering 230hp at 8800rpm from just 1995cc, it had one of the highest specific power outputs of any

Conceived as a way to homologate the 33 for racing, the 33 Stradale is widely recognised as one of the most beautiful car designs of all time.

Plastic bodywork helped keep weight ultra-low – just 700kg overall

Despite only being 1995cc in capacity, the V8 engine produced 230hp at 8800rpm – good enough for a 160mph top speed.

naturally aspirated V8 ever made. In Stradale form, it was fully capable of exceeding 160mph.

A small independent outfit called Carrozzeria Marazzi built the car, and Scaglione himself personally inspected each example before delivery. The 33 Stradale made its debut at the 1967 Sports Car Show at Monza race circuit. This was also an exceedingly expensive machine: in 1968, it cost 9,750,000 lire, at a time when a Lamborghini Miura was a mere 7,700,000 lire. Unsurprisingly, then, that of the 50 examples originally planned, only 18 chassis were ultimately manufactured.

A highly innovative slice of design was the "scissor" door arrangement.

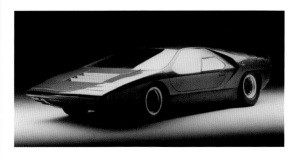

Bertone's stunning 33-based Carabo of 1968.

Tasteful Italdesign Iguana of 1969.

Pininfarina P33 Roadster was an aerodynamic pioneer.

1969 Pininfarina 33 coupé Prototipo Speciale copied the previous year's Ferrari 250 P5.

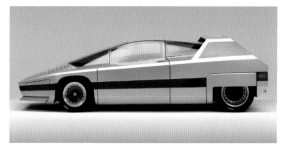

Extreme wedge: Pininfarina's 1971 33 Spider Cuneo.

The Bertone Navajo did not debut until 1976.

BEYOND EXOTIC

Of the 18 Alfa 33 Stradale chassis made, six were passed on to independent carrozzerie for them to make exotic concept cars. The first to appear (chassis number 75033.109) was Bertone's Carabo at the Paris Show in October 1968. Its distinctive wedge shape, created by Marcello Gandini, was claimed to maximise downforce, and like the 33 Stradale, it had scissor-opening doors and sat just 990mm (39 inches) high. Distinctive louvres on the engine cover were replicated in the design of the three separate pop-up slats over the headlights.

One month later, at the November 1968 Turin Show, Pininfarina unveiled its P33 Roadster (chassis number 75033.108). Another wedge-shaped creation, it was an open sports-racer style. One of the highlights was an aerofoil behind the seats which doubled up as a rollover bar and oil cooler, and whose angle could be adjusted to boost downforce, something that the front flaps could also do. A row of six headlights was mounted under a movable plastic cover.

At Paris in 1969 came Pininfarina's 33 coupé Prototipo Speciale, which pretty much duplicated the shape of the previous year's Ferrari 250 P5 but sat on an Alfa 33/2 chassis (number 75033.115). What a shape it was: curvaceous, lithe, sporting gullwing doors and even quite practical. Pininfarina suggested there might be a production run but sadly that proved to be pie in the sky.

At the Turin Show of November 1969, Giugiaro's newly founded Italdesign produced the Iguana (on chassis number 75033.116). Not perhaps as dramatic as the other 33-based concepts, it nevertheless pointed the way for future Giugiaro supercars.

The next 33-based car appeared at the 1971 Brussels Show: Pininfarina's 33 Spider (sometimes called Cuneo). Extremely wedgy in shape, it had a certain Formula 1 influence. The very last 33 concept did not arrive until the 1976 Geneva Show, when Bertone's clothing of chassis number 75033.117 was unveiled: the Navajo. Expressing peak 1970s wedginess, it featured rigidly squared-off shapes.

The production Montreal, launched in 1970, looked different because it was redesigned around V8 power.

MONTREAL (1970-1977)

There is no Alfa Romeo quite like the Montreal, treading as it does the fine line between art and machine. Regarding the former, the artist behind its unique lines was Marcello Gandini, who in 1967 was employed at Bertone's design studio. His initial design work on the Montreal – so named because it was first seen at the 1967 Expo in Montreal, Canada – was rather different to the eventual car you could buy, with more curvaceous and, some might say, more harmonious lines. So overwhelmingly positive was the public reaction to Bertone's coupé that Alfa Romeo was persuaded that it should develop a production version.

Easily the most striking design element was the sequence of slots in the C-pillar, which suggested a mid-mounted engine. In fact, the powerplant was placed up front. In the original '67 show car, this was a 1.6-litre four-cylinder engine, taken straight from the Giulia; indeed, the whole car was based on a pretty much standard Tipo 105 Giulia floorpan. However, Alfa decided to make the production Montreal a much more upmarket model by switching to V8 power – a decision that caused controversy both inside Alfa Romeo, and between Alfa Romeo and Bertone. Bertone knew that incorporating a bulky V8 in its design would mean moving the entire powertrain back in the chassis, entailing several compromises, but

As originally shown at the 1967 Montreal Expo, the Montreal prototype had a four-cylinder Giulia engine.

The 2593cc engine was an enlarged but detuned (200hp)
version of the 33's V8.

To drive, the Montreal felt lively, capable of 140mph and
0-60mph in 7.5 seconds.

Marcello Gandini of Bertone was responsible for the Montreal's unique shape.

Alfa Romeo ignored Bertone's arguments. The change to V8 power radically altered the original design.

The V8 engine was an enlarged 2593cc detuned version of the Tipo 33's 90-degree V8. It retained an essentially race car spec, including wet liners in an aluminium block, aluminium heads, four chain-driven camshafts, sodium-filled exhaust valves, a dry-sump oil system and Spica mechanical fuel injection. Pumping out 200hp at 6500rpm, this was quite a lively machine, able to reach just shy of 140mph,

and do 0-60mph in 7.5 seconds. Unfortunately, however, the racing-derived V8 didn't acquire a reputation for 100% reliability in regular road use.

The ZF five-speed manual gearbox fed power to a ZF limited-slip differential mounted in, perhaps surprisingly for such an exotic machine, a rather antiquated live axle set-up. An anti-roll bar helped reduce body roll and, together with double wishbones up front, the car handled reasonably well, in keeping with its principal role as a grand tourer more than

Essentially based on a Giulia 105 platform, the Montreal handled more like a grand tourer than a sports car.

Driver-focused dashboard featured in what was really a 2+2 cabin.

an out-and-out sports car. Braking was by ventilated discs all round.

Inside, the dashboard was strikingly designed with two binnacles housing all the instrumentation. Most of the switchgear was confined to the centre console, including heating and air conditioning (when fitted; it was optional until becoming standard in 1972). The relatively short wheelbase meant that, although there was seating for four, the rear passengers didn't have an awful lot of room.

The series production Montreal debuted at the Geneva Motor Show in 1970, three years after the original concept had been shown. The overall styling had been somewhat watered down, although it kept the distinctive "air slots" behind each door and louvred covers over the headlights.

The press didn't particularly like the new car, which proved to be a controversial addition to Alfa's range. The problem was that the Montreal was priced at exotic car levels: at 5,200,000 lire, it was twice as much as a Giulia 2000 GTV, yet in essence its underpinnings were still derived from the humble Giulia.

The chassis felt overwhelmed by the V8 engine, while the car's grand touring capabilities were not helped by its lack of power steering, making low-speed manoeuvring a real chore.

The Montreal never really lived up to its early promise and unfortunately it spent most of its production life languishing in an oil crisis. Up until 1977, when production ceased, a mere 3925 examples were made, 180 of which had right-hand drive.

SPECIFICATIONS

MONTREAL

Engine:	2593cc V8 twin-cam
Power:	200hp @ 6500rpm
Torque:	243Nm (179lb ft) @ 5100rpm
Transmission:	5-speed manual
Wheels:	14in alloy
Weight:	1330kg
Max speed:	136mph
0-62mph:	8.0sec

Chapter Seven

ALFETTA TIPO 116:
BETTER THE ALFETTA

The Tipo 116 Alfetta saloon was named after the racing car which shared its transaxle mechanical layout.

When it came to naming Alfa Romeo's new saloon car in 1972, the name almost chose itself. The Alfetta borrowed its moniker from the legendary Alfa Romeo racer of the 1940s that had enjoyed such competition success. But why name a saloon after a Grand Prix car? Simple: the new car adopted the old racer's layout of a rear-mounted transaxle, where the transmission and final drive are in unit with the rear axle. Such a set-up was unlike any other car then being made.

The Alfetta was Dr Orazio Satta's last major new model for Alfa Romeo prior to his death in 1974.

And since his time at Alfa stretched right back to the Alfetta 158/159 Grand Prix era, he was able to draw directly on his experiences of the transaxle layout from those triumphant cars.

Prototypes of the new transaxle car were running as early as July 1968 and displayed great potential in terms of roadholding and handling, since the weight distribution could be made near-perfect 50/50 front/rear. However, there were also significant challenges to overcome in terms of the gearchange, gearbox and steering. Delays in development – much of them caused by Alfa Romeo launching another highly significant new

model, the Alfasud – meant that the Tipo 116 Alfetta did not make its public debut until May 1972.

In marketing terms, the new Alfetta saloon slotted in between the Giulia 1300/1600 and the top-of-the-range 2000 Berlina. Pretty much the engine was the only item that was not all-new, being taken direct from the 1750, with only the sump, exhaust manifolds and cooling equipment altered.

The front suspension was new for Alfa Romeo, consisting of double wishbones, longitudinal torsion bars (a first for Alfa, replacing the more conventional springs) and an anti-roll bar. The rear end was even more unusual. The gearbox, clutch, differential and brakes were effectively mounted in a single sprung unit. The entirely new gearbox had five speeds, and it was very unusual for it to be combined with the final drive unit at the rear, while the clutch was also located at the rear of the car. The rear brake discs were fitted inboard, on either side of the differential. The rear suspension was by de Dion axle, progressive-rate coil springs, Watt linkage and anti-roll bar. Conventional telescopic dampers were used all round, while the steering was rack-and-pinion.

The upsides to the transaxle format were manifold: perfect front-to-rear weight distribution and therefore better handling balance, plus less unsprung weight

due to the rear disc brakes being mounted inboard, alongside the differential. However, there were also disadvantages. The propshaft rotated at the same speed as the engine, with obvious connotations for noise, vibration and harshness. In order to reduce vibration, the propshaft was split into two, with rubber couplings mounted between each section – a solution that worked remarkably well. Another disadvantage was the awkward gear linkage, meaning the transmission was not always as slick-shifting as it should be.

It was not until 1974 that the coupé version of the Tipo 116 – called the Alfetta GT – arrived, using the saloon's platform shortened by 110mm in the wheelbase. Initially fitted with the 1779cc engine, it soon changed to 1.6 power, as well as the definitive 2.0-litre engine that would see it through to the end of its production life. 1980 also saw the arrival of something very significant: the glorious 2.5-litre "Busso" GTV 6 which saw the Alfetta range reach its zenith.

The GTV was axed in 1986, with no direct successor. Apart from the existing, much smaller Alfasud Sprint (see Chapter 9), it would not be until the new GTV of 1994 that Alfa Romeo would again have a four-seater coupé in its line-up. A grand total of 137,579 examples of the GT and GTV were made in a 12-year lifespan.

The Alfetta saloon slotted into Alfa's range above the Giulia 1300/1600 but below the 2000 Berlina.

The Alfetta GT was a Giugiaro design quite unlike anything else he was doing in the 1970s.

ALFETTA GT 1.8 (1974-1976), GT 1.6 (1976-1980) & GTV 2.0 (1976-1986)

It was fitting that the designer called upon to create the successor to the Giulia Sprint GT should be Giorgetto Giugiaro. Now an independent designer (having created his own company in 1968, which would eventually be named Italdesign), for the coupé version of the Alfetta Giugiaro created a very different sort of car than his early 1960s original.

However, since he designed the new coupé some years before it eventually reached the market in 1974, the GT already felt like an ageing design at launch.

It certainly suffered in comparison to Giugiaro's latest "folded paper" school of thought, initiated with the VW Passat in 1973 and VW Golf in 1974, which became so influential, and many thought the Alfetta GT a throwback to an older style.

The remit had been to make a full four-seater coupé, and that meant keeping the roofline high, resulting in Giugiaro selecting a fastback style. It was elegant in its own way, and certainly an aerodynamic shape for the time, with a Cd figure of 0.39, notably employing a small front spoiler and a chopped-off Kamm tail. Design details included four front lights, metal bumpers with rubber inserts and distinctive air

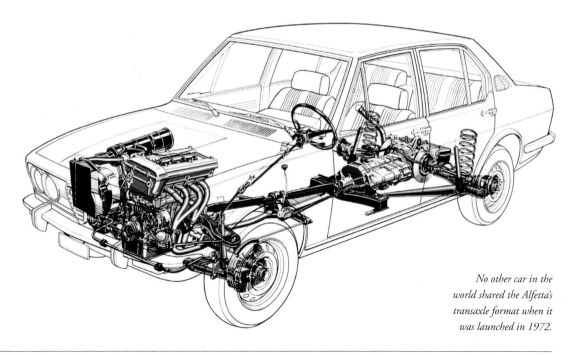

No other car in the world shared the Alfetta's transaxle format when it was launched in 1972.

vent louvres in the C-pillars.

Inside the car was a rather bizarre dashboard layout. The rev counter was mounted in a square binnacle directly in front of the driver, with the speedometer and other gauges located in a separate central binnacle. This attracted a lot of criticism and eventually Alfa relented and replaced it with an all-new dash with the main instruments repositioned ahead of the driver.

This was a four-seater coupé, but while there was generous space up front, there was rather less in the back, partly because the rear seats sat so high in order to clear the transaxle. At least the rear passengers got winding windows, albeit not very large ones. Perhaps surprisingly, the rear seats could not be folded down to boost space in the boot – which was accessed via something of a novelty for a coupé at the time: a full-sized opening tailgate (or hatchback).

The Alfetta GT was launched with just one 1.8-litre engine option. Since the old Bertone 2000 GTV was still on sale, Alfa wanted to distinguish the two models, which explains why it didn't use the 2.0-litre engine initially. The venerable 1779cc Alfa twin-cam engine with its two Weber 40 carbs developed a healthy 122hp at 5500rpm, and could do 0-60mph in under 10 seconds.

Motor Sport magazine loved the way it drove: "The precision of steering feels to shrink this car through gaps where slab-sided, compact family cars would fear to tread." And while the suspension was soft, "whatever the body angle each corner, it refuses to forsake the tarmac," adding that the GT was, "a much less nervous car in corners than earlier Alfas, adding a large enough margin of safety and stability to keep less

The GT was available in just one guise at launch, with a 1.8-litre engine.

This cutaway clearly shows the rear-mounted gearbox and inboard rear brake discs.

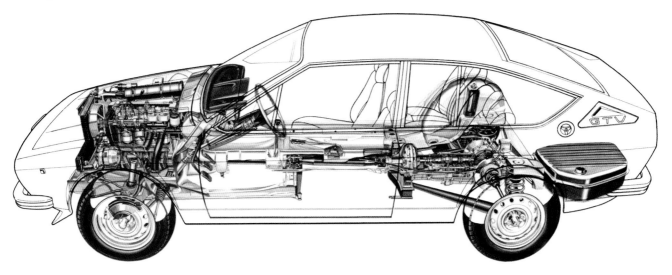

The Alfetta GT marked a definite move upwards in terms of driving sophistication compared to the Giulia GT.

Rear end featured a practical hatchback. This is a rare 1979 GTS special edition.

able drivers out of trouble up to extraordinarily high cornering speeds."

But the same review was scathing about the gearchange: "It is notchy, it is baulky, particularly into first and second into which cogs the test car sometimes needed an extraordinary amount of force, it is out-of-keeping with the thoroughbred spirit of the rest of the running gear. The gearchange is clunkily noisy, too."

When the old Bertone Tipo 105 coupé finally died, Alfa replaced the 1779cc Alfetta GT in May 1976 with two new models: the 1.6 and 2.0, with 109hp and 122hp respectively, the latter earning the name GTV. The GTV's 4.1:1 final drive ratio remained the same as the old 1.8-litre GT's, while the 1.6 GT was fitted with a lower 4.3:1 ratio to maintain keen acceleration. Distinguishing the GTV were bumper

overriders, different wheels, "GTV" lettering carved into the C-pillar air vents and a wooden dashboard.

Motor Sport also tested a 2.0-litre GTV in 1977

SPECIFICATIONS	
GT 1.8	
Engine:	1779cc 4-cyl twin-cam
Power:	122hp @ 5500rpm (118hp from 1975)
Torque:	167Nm (123lb ft) @ 4400rpm
Transmission:	5-speed manual
Wheels:	14in steel or alloy
Weight:	1054kg
Max speed:	118mph
0-62mph:	10.0sec

and said: "If the twin-cam Alfa engine is becoming long in the tooth, age has not detracted from its personality. True, the long stroke makes it feel a little rough by contemporary standards, but it makes up for this by a wide spread of torque, tractability, power and docility."

In 1979, the 2.0 engine was lightly revised with new camshaft profiles and better ignition advance, resulting in a healthier 130hp power output and a

redesignation as the Alfetta GTV 2000L. In 1980 came a revised Series 2 model, which dropped the Alfetta name in favour of simply "GTV". The 1.6-litre engine was also dropped at this point, leaving only the 2.0-litre (plus the new GTV 6 – see below). The old stainless steel bumpers and brightwork were replaced by black/grey plastic bumper covers and matt-black trim. The rear lights were also redesigned, becoming one single unit, while

After 1976, the 1.8 engine was dropped in favour of 2.0 power or – as seen here – 1.6 litres.

S P E C I F I C A T I O N S	
GT 1.6	
Engine:	1570cc 4-cyl twin-cam
Power:	109hp @ 5600rpm
Torque:	141Nm (104lb ft) @ 4300rpm
Transmission:	5-speed manual
Wheels:	14in steel or alloy
Weight:	1080kg
Max speed:	111mph
0-62mph:	11.0sec

S P E C I F I C A T I O N S	
GTV 2.0	
Engine:	1962cc 4-cyl twin-cam
Power	122hp at 5300rpm (130hp from 1979)
Torque	176Nm (129lb ft) @ 4000rpm
Transmission	5-speed manual
Wheels	14in or 15in steel or alloy
Weight	1080kg
Max speed	121mph
0-62mph	9.5sec

The 2.0-litre GTV was readily identifiable by its "GTV" lettering on the C-pillar.

The early GT dashboard was eccentric, featuring a rev counter ahead of the driver and an offset speedometer.

The GT was facelifted for the 1980s with black trim almost entirely replacing brightwork.

the spoiler was also reprofiled. Inside was a much more conventional dashboard that did away with the separate binnacles in favour of one large binnacle with all the main instruments ahead of the driver and minor gauges towards the centre of the dash.

In February 1983 came another minor facelift, notably adding contrasting-colour plastic lower flanks, while inside were new seats and upholstery.

By the time production ended in 1986, a total of 21,947 Alfetta GT 1.8s had been made, plus 16,923 1.6-litre GTs, and 75,023 2.0-litre GTVs (31,267 from 1976–1978, 26,108 L models 1979–1980, 10,352 Series 2 1980–1983 and 7296 facelift cars 1983–1987).

The 1979 Alfetta GTV 2000 Turbodelta was Italy's first ever production turbocharged car.

A gloriously radiant colour scheme identified the Turbodelta.

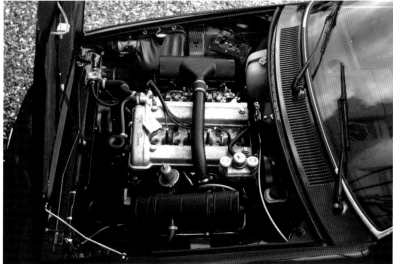

A KKK turbo ensured 150hp of power and 230Nm (170lb ft) of torque.

ALFETTA GTV 2.0 TURBODELTA (1979-1980)

1979 saw Carlo Chiti's Autodelta turbocharge the 2.0-litre GTV to produce the Turbodelta, an FIA homologation special aimed at Group 4 rally competition. This was the very first Italian production car ever fitted with a turbo. The Turbodelta road-going model had a single KKK turbocharger, new pistons, cylinder liners and camshafts. Changes were also made to the exhaust, radiator, clutch and dampers. Power output grew to 150hp, but more significant to the driving experience was the leap in torque to 230Nm (170lb ft).

The only exterior changes were a louvre on each side of the black-painted bonnet and some deliciously lairy body side stripes realised in yellow, orange, red and blue, with the word Turbodelta inscribed on the doors.

Only 400 examples were made from 1979 to 1980, some of which were given fuel injection instead of twin carburettors by the German Alfa Romeo importer. The Turbodelta's niche was squeezed out by the arrival, in 1980, of the V6-powered GTV 6.

SPECIFICATIONS	
GTV 2.0 TURBODELTA	
Engine:	1962cc 4-cyl twin-cam turbo
Power:	150hp at 5500rpm
Torque:	230Nm (170lb ft) @ 3500rpm
Transmission:	5-speed manual
Wheels:	14in steel or alloy
Weight:	1080kg
Max speed:	121mph
0-62mph:	9.5sec

The Alfetta GTV 6 2.5 was one of the world's great four-seater coupés in the 1980s.

Apart from V6 power, mechanical changes included wider tyres on 15-inch wheels, revised suspension and stronger driveshafts.

ALFETTA GTV 6 2.5 (1980-1986)

At the same time as the Series 2 GTV was launched in 1980, a significant new range-topper arrived: the GTV 6. This was only the second ever car to receive Alfa's magnificent Giuseppe Busso-designed 2.5-litre V6 (following the 1979 Alfa 6 saloon). Unusually for Alfa Romeo, the six cylinders were arranged in a 60-degree vee; all previous Alfa sixes had been in-line.

The all-aluminium V6 had over-square dimensions (88mm bore, 68.3mm stroke) and two belt-driven camshafts. As fitted to the GTV, Bosch L-Jetronic fuel injection replaced the Alfa 6's troublesome carburettors, and it produced a healthy 160hp at 5600rpm. Other mechanical changes included a new twin-plate clutch, a taller fifth gear, upgraded brakes (utilising

Body side cladding was part of a range-wide minor facelift in 1983.

The 2.5 GTV 6 was a very popular model in the Alfetta range.

Along with other Series 2 Alfettas, the GTV 6 received a more conventional dash.

In tests, the GTV 6 achieved a 0–60mph time of 8.8 seconds and a top speed of 132mph.

Heart of the GTV 6 was the glorious Busso-designed V6 engine, which gave 160hp.

ventilated discs up front), wider 195/65 tyres on 15-inch rims, larger fuel tank, revised suspension and stronger driveshafts. Meanwhile, to clear the V6, the bonnet gained a power bulge with an air vent in it.

The Busso V6 was a wonderfully free-revving engine that revelled in a glorious exhaust note. Road testers raved about it, with *Road & Track* saying: "It makes those great Italian ripping-raw-fabric sounds, has lots of torque and sends the car down the road smartly."

Autocar magazine achieved a 0–60mph time of 8.8 seconds and a top speed of 132mph. The heavier V6 engine did engender a little more understeer than the lighter four-cylinder GTV, but the inherent balance of the transaxle layout kept its well-sorted handling on song.

S P E C I F I C A T I O N S	
GTV 6 2.5	
Engine:	2492cc V6-cyl twin-cam
Power:	160hp at 5600rpm
Torque:	213Nm (157lb ft) @ 4000rpm
Transmission:	5-speed manual
Wheels:	15in alloy
Weight	1080kg
Max speed:	132mph
0-62mph:	8.8sec

GTV8 of 1977 had a 200hp Montreal V8 engine, engineered by Autodelta in Italy but sold only in Germany.

Capable of 143mph, only three GTV8s were made as it was so expensive.

South African buyers were treated to a 3.0-litre V6 GTV.

The Autodelta-engineered 3.0 conversion produced 174hp.

With a 0-60mph time of 8.4 seconds and a 139mph top speed, the GTV 3.0 V6 was perfect for racing.

AFFECTED ALFETTAS

The GTV inspired specialists across the world to produce a whole raft of hotted-up "specials". We'll concentrate on the official and semi-official ones here, starting with Alfa Romeo's distributor in Germany, which offered a V8-engined GTV8 in 1977, powered by a 200hp Montreal lump. The conversion was engineered by Autodelta in Italy and the resulting machine could do 0-62mph in 7.5 seconds and reach a top speed of 143mph. However, just three GTV8s were built, since its list price was fully twice as much as a regular GTV.

In the late 1970s, one of the UK's best-known Alfa Romeo dealers, Bell & Colvill, produced its own GTV Turbo model for domestic consumption, using a Garrett turbo that kicked out around 175hp. There was an even more extreme turbo variant in the USA. The twin-turbo Callaway GTV 6 was a real beast, offering 230hp. Some 36 examples were built between 1983 and 1986.

The GTV 6 proved very successful in competition, for instance winning the British Touring Car Championship outright and gaining class wins in European Touring Cars. But in South Africa, the 2.5-litre GTV 6 simply wasn't powerful enough to compete with the BMWs that were dominating Group 1 racing, so in 1984 the local importer beat a path to Autodelta (Alfa's competition department), which was already offering a 3.0-litre conversion. The result was an official 3.0-litre V6 model exclusively for the South African market. New cylinder heads, crankshafts and pistons were assembled in South Africa and mated to six carburettors. Other changes to the GTV 3.0 V6 included lowered suspension, a larger front spoiler, glassfibre bonnet with cooling vent, Compomotive split-rim alloy wheels and Recaro seats. Power was now up to 174hp, enough to see off BMWs in racing; the 0-60mph time dropped to 8.4sec, and top speed rose to 139mph. Slightly more than 200 GTV 3.0 V6s were made in South Africa from 1984 to 1985.

Chapter Eight

ES-30:

IL MOSTRO

Brutal; race-inspired; hand-built; exclusive – the Alfa Romeo SZ was all of these things. It could also be described – and was in no uncertain terms – as hideously ugly. But as an end-of-an-era swansong at Alfa Romeo, the SZ was unquestionably a spectacular machine.

Alfa Romeo had replaced its Alfetta saloon with the new 75 back in 1985, even though underneath it remained pretty much the same as the old Alfetta, complete with its rear-mounted transaxle. Production of the 75 continued right up until 1992, by which time nearly 387,000 examples had found owners. But the 75 was not the end of the transaxle era at Alfa; the 75-based SZ coupé and RZ convertible would keep the flag flying right up until 1994.

When the SZ was unveiled at the 1989 Geneva

Six headlamps and design aggression encapsulated: the monster awakes.

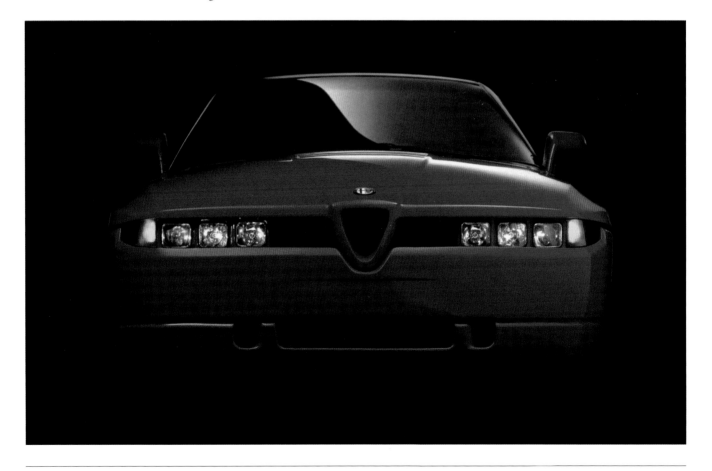

The SZ was built by Zagato but designed in-house at Alfa Romeo by a team headed by Robert Opron.

Motor Show, it was presented as the "Experimental Sportscar 3.0-litre" (or ES-30). The official name SZ would come later. The Z in SZ referred to Zagato, the Milanese coachbuilder, and while Zagato built the new car, it absolutely did not design it. Instead, it was created by a team of Fiat Group insiders, headed by Robert Opron (designer of the Citroen SM), with much of the actual design work done by a talented man at Centro Stile called Antonio Castellana. The SZ was, incidentally, one the first cars ever to be entirely designed using CAD (computer-aided design).

The SZ had so many unusual design features. The six-light front end was provocative to say the least. The bonnet featured ribs that appeared to be cooling vents but were in fact purely decorative. The upright windscreen was tortuously curved, contrasting with a dramatically swooping roofline that was truncated by a genuine carbonfibre rear spoiler – one of the first uses of carbon in a road car. The design may have looked from some angles like an awkwardly butchered off-cut of meat but that belied its wind-tunnel smooth aerodynamics (it had a drag coefficient of just 0.30). There was no question that it was brutal; some thought it hideous, others one of the most charismatic shapes

of modern times. *Car* magazine called it "Ugly as sin and just as tempting". As for the Italians, they nicknamed it "Il Mostro" – The Monster.

No other car company, before or since, had ever used the peculiar type of plastic (ICI Modar) that Alfa Romeo chose to craft the body out of. The decision did cause problems, as the paint had a hard time sticking to the body, resulting in a deluge of warranty claims over bubbling paintwork. Every single SZ was painted red with a contrasting dark grey roof – well, all except the one belonging to the head of Zagato at the time, Andrea Zagato, which was painted black.

Inside, the quirkiness continued, with exposed painted panels, light tan leather seats and a dashboard that looked like it had been hewn from carbonfibre (it was in fact stick-on faux-carbon). Behind the two seats was an area reserved for luggage, with straps to keep your bags in place. Alfa Romeo might have put seats here – there was certainly enough room to fit small seats in – but the fact was there was nowhere else to put luggage; the bottom-hinged "boot lid" was nothing of the sort and simply provided access to the space saver spare wheel.

Underneath, the SZ was essentially an Alfa Romeo 75 racer. It used the coilover front suspension from

Highly unusual shape featured a deep front end and an extremely curved windscreen.

Sharply cut-off tail was surmounted by a carbonfibre spoiler – one of the first times a production car had ever used carbon.

Cabin was a mix of stripped-back focus and leather luxury.

SZ looks more aggressive on 18-inch wheels, as here – 16 inches were standard.

the 75 Group A/IMSA racer, rather than the standard road 75's torsion bars. Anti-roll bars were fitted all round, along with specially-developed Koni hydraulic dampers that allowed the driver to raise the car by 50mm using switches in the centre console – handy when overcoming sleeping policemen. The rear-mounted five-speed transaxle and de Dion tube give it near-ideal weight distribution (56% front, 44% rear), while the inboard rear disc brakes reduced unsprung weight. The SZ used ventilated disc brakes all round, but Alfa chose not to fit ABS to give the car a true race vibe. 16-inch Speedline wheels were shod with

Fabulous 3.0-litre Busso V6 engine used special components to squeeze out 210hp.

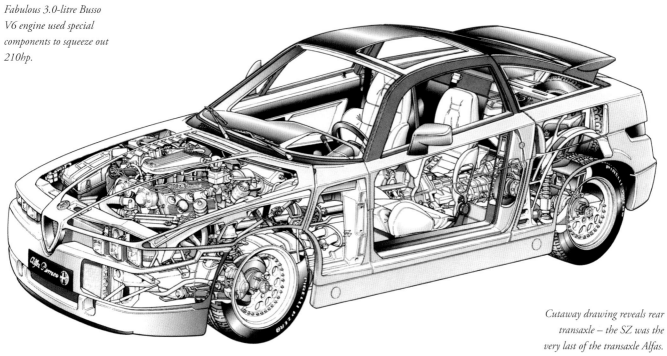

Cutaway drawing reveals rear transaxle – the SZ was the very last of the transaxle Alfas.

RZ was the "Roadster Zagato" follow-up to the SZ coupé.

205/55 front tyres and 225/50 rears, giving it huge grip; indeed, Alfa Romeo famously claimed the SZ was capable of pulling 1.4g in corners.

The SZ used an uprated development of the 75 3.0-litre Busso V6 engine. Despite Alfa tweaking the fuel injection, camshaft timing, compression ratio and uprating the intake and exhaust manifolds of the 2959cc V6, its power output was perhaps a disappoint-

ment for the price (the SZ cost around £40,000 when new). Peak power was 210hp at 6200rpm, and torque was 245Nm (181lb ft) at 4500rpm. Still, this was a fast car that some classed in the supercar category, with a 0-62mph time of around seven seconds and a top speed of 152mph.

The SZ was assembled at Zagato's Milan plant. The first 11 examples left the factory in 1989, with

Almost all the RZ's body panels were different from the SZ's. Loss of rigidity affected handling somewhat.

Interior differed from SZ in its all-black colour scheme, white dials and "floating" rear console.

a further 289 following in 1990 and the final 736 in 1991, making a grand total of 1036 cars, all of which were left-hand drive.

That might well have been that for Il Mostro, but Zagato had other ideas. It proposed a convertible model called the RZ (Roadster Zagato), which was – unlike the SZ – designed by Zagato itself. The RZ had numerous differences: the front bumper was shallower, as were the body sills; the doors were frameless at the top; the windscreen was lower; and the bonnet lacked the SZ's faux vents. The biggest difference, though, was the fabric roof, hidden beneath an elegant double-bubble rear deck when folded. Inside, the dashboard was plain black, housing white-faced dials, and there was a "floating" rear console between the seats. In contrast to the red-only SZ, the RZ could be ordered painted red with a black interior, yellow with black interior or black with burgundy interior.

There was a certain loss of rigidity after chopping the roof off, leading to scuttle shake and woollier handling than the super-sharp SZ. Today, enthusiasts tend to prefer the SZ coupé to the RZ, but the latter's rarity does give it kudos: only 278 RZs were made between 1992 and 1994, or about a quarter of the number of SZs. Today, Il Mostro in either open or closed forms has an almost mythical status; whether you love it or hate it – or sometimes both – it has an undeniable aura that makes it one of the world's most exceptional cars.

The RZ was much rarer than the SZ, but tends to be less favoured by collectors today.

SPECIFICATIONS	
SZ/RZ	
Engine:	2959cc V6 twin-cam
Power:	210hp @ 6200rpm
Torque:	245Nm (181lb ft) @ 4500rpm
Transmission:	5-speed manual transaxle
Wheels:	16in alloy
Weight:	1256kg/1380kg
Top speed:	152mph
0-62mph:	7.0sec

Chapter Nine

NEW ERA:

FRONT-WHEEL DRIVE & SPORTING REBIRTH

The final chapter of this book is given over to Alfa's "new era" coupés and spiders: the Alfasud (its first ever front-drive model); Tipo 916; GT; Brera/Spider (the first sporting Alfa offered with 4x4); 4C and 8C.

ALFASUD SPRINT (1976-1989)

The story of the Alfasud starts when the Italian Government – which effectively owned Alfa Romeo – insisted that the company's new small car for the

1970s should be built in Italy's depressed south to boost employment there (hence the name, Alfa "sud" or "south"). This new popular family model would share almost nothing with any existing Alfa model, and the significant challenge of creating it was given to the newly hired Rudolf Hruska, the Austrian engineer who had previously worked for Abarth, Porsche and Fiat. Giugiaro's newly formed design house, Italdesign, not only did the car's styling but also its packaging and body engineering. Between

The Alfasud Sprint family lasted in production for 13 years, over several evolutionary phases.

Hruska and Giugiaro, the job done on the Alfasud was widely greeted as a triumph.

Launched in 1971, this was Alfa's first ever front-wheel drive production car. An all-new flat-four "boxer" engine was developed, using a gearbox mounted directly behind it. The rear suspension was by solid beam (which also doubled as an anti-roll bar), cleverly located by Watt linkages: all very compact and contributing much to the Alfasud's legendary handling and ride. Up front were MacPherson struts and coil springs, while in-board front brakes lowered the overall unsprung weight. Among the many positives of the Alfasud were extraordinary handling, a super-sweet engine, great packaging and an excellent ride.

The platform having excited a new generation of

Giugiaro's Italdesign did the Sprint's styling over an Alfasud saloon platform.

Plaudits rained in on the Sprint's drivability: this was a crisp-handling, high-performing coupé.

Interior design was smart and ergonomic. Seating was really only for 2+2 passengers.

Flat-four engine took up very little space indeed, and also sat low down, to the benefit of handling.

Rear end featured a handy tailgate. This is a 1.5 Sprint Veloce.

hot hatch lovers, it was entirely logical for Alfa Romeo to develop a coupé version, known as the Alfasud Sprint. Giugiaro was again called on to do the design work, and he mixed styling cues from the Alfetta GT and his Volkswagen Scirocco to create a very crisp shape. Built on the Alfasud saloon floorpan, the Sprint was slightly stiffer overall but carried an extra 80kg of weight. Although the rear seats were more suitable for children than adults, the boot, accessed through a hatchback, was a decent size.

Launched in Italy in September 1976, the initial Alfasud Sprint 1.3 had a 1286cc engine – the most

Many versions of the Sprint were offered; this is a Trofeo edition from 1982, named after Alfa's one-make Trofeo racer.

Towards the end of its life, the Sprint was also sold in upmarket Quadrifoglio Verde form.

In 1983, the range was renamed simply Sprint (no longer Alfasud) and got a facelift.

potent Alfasud engine at that time, with 76hp and 76lb ft of torque. Extra power came in 1978 when the 1.3 engine was enlarged to 1351cc to give 79hp, while a new 1490cc Sprint 1.5 with 85hp was also introduced. The following year, Veloce versions offered even more power (86hp and 95hp respectively).

Despite the Alfasud being replaced by the 33 in 1983, the Sprint continued in production as the Alfa Romeo Sprint (losing its Alfasud badging). The 1.5 Veloce was transformed to become the Sprint Green Cloverleaf with 105hp on tap and substantial cosmetic changes. A final round of engine and trim mods came

A rather ungainly bodykit and rear spoiler featured on late QV models.

Very 1980s feel for the post-1987 Sprint cabin.

at the end of 1987 when the Sprint inherited the 33's mechanical components, including its 118hp 1712cc engine. Some 121,434 Sprints had been made by the time production ended in 1989, making it one of Alfa's most successful coupés ever.

SPECIFICATIONS	
SPRINT 1.5 GREEN CLOVERLEAF	
Engine:	1490cc flat-four
Power:	105hp @ 5800rpm
Torque:	133Nm (98lb ft) @ 5000rpm
Transmission:	5-speed manual
Wheels:	14in alloy
Weight:	915kg
Top Speed:	115mph
0-62mph:	11.2sec

The Tipo 916 range, seen here from early Spider/GTV to later Cup and facelifted models.

GTV & SPIDER TIPO 916 (1994-2006)

The Tipo 916 GTV and Spider twins had a long gestation period. The project was initiated in 1987, with prototypes built the following year basically being identical in shape to the eventual production car, but it took fully seven years for the Tipo 916 to reach the market. The reasons were many, not least being that Fiat, the new boss of Alfa Romeo (having taken Alfa over in 1986), developed its own Fiat coupé on the same platform, and brought that to market first.

The man tasked with designing the new Alfa Romeo was Enrico Fumia of Pininfarina, who had previously styled the acclaimed Alfa 164 saloon. His work on the new coupé and spider was extraordinary. The front end was dominated by a dramatic clamshell bonnet made of composite material, punctured with apertures for the grille and lights. A deep swage line ran from the front wheelarch to below the rear window, while the cut-off rear end with its full-width light panel was equally dramatic.

The GTV and Spider used the same platform as Fiat's 1989 European Car of the Year winner, the Fiat Tipo, although very few components were in fact directly shared. The multi-link rear suspension,

Despite being Alfa Romeo's first front-wheel drive V6 sports car, the GTV was praised for its sporty handling.

Pininfarina's design for the GTV was audacious, its steeply raked swage line being very notable.

for instance, was specific to the Alfa, mounted in a subframe, with a small amount of rear-wheel steering built in. Braking was by vented discs front and rear.

The GTV and Spider were launched simultaneously at the 1994 Paris Motor Show. Two engines were sold in the UK to start with: the 2.0-litre Twin Spark (150hp) and 3.0-litre Busso V6 (220hp). The Italian market also got a turbocharged 2.0-litre V6 (202hp) for tax reasons. Some European markets also

got a 1.8-litre engine, plus a 190hp V6, but not the UK. From 2003, the V6 engine was expanded to 3.2 litres (and power rose to 240hp), while the 2.0-litre evolved to JTS spec (with 165hp). The GTV/Spider transmission was only ever manual.

While the GTV was a 2+2 seater – albeit not a very practical one, having tiny rear seats and an almost non-existent boot – the Spider was a strict two-seater, whose folding soft-top hid neatly under a

Rear end was dominated by Kamm-shape tail and, in some versions, a spoiler.

Gorgeous-looking cabin was easy to use, but Alfa's claim of 2+2 seating was overstated.

The 916 Spider looked every bit as arresting as the GTV.

When folded, the roof stowed away under a neat tonneau cover.

Dual-cowl instrument binnacle drew inspiration from classic Alfa Spiders.

Alfa's latest 2.0 JTS petrol four-cylinder engine arrived in 2003, offering 165hp.

Limited edition GTV Cup sported unique bodykit and front wing vents.　　　*Very few Cup models were made, making this the most desirable 916 variant today.*

solid tonneau when pulled down.

Two facelifts occurred, the first (Phase II) a minor one in 1998, followed by a more major one (Phase III) in 2003, adopting an Alfa 147-inspired front grille. Undoubtedly the most desirable model of all was the limited edition Cup, which had spoilers front and rear, side skirts, front wing vents, titanium-finish 17-inch alloy wheels, leather upholstery and a numbered plaque.

The GTV was replaced in 2005 by the Brera, with the Spider soldiering on for one more year until its Brera-based successor arrived. A total of 81,799 examples of the 916 twins were built, with the production split approximately 41,800 GTVs and 39,000 Spiders. Pininfarina's shape has certainly aged well and, despite the controversies surrounding front-wheel drive in an Alfa sports car, the 916 has a strong enthusiast base today.

Many buyers preferred the Busso 3.0 V6 engine. Note the oblong headlamps – it was the bonnet's cut-outs that gave the twin round lamp look.

SPECIFICATIONS

GTV 3.0 V6

Engine:	Engine: 2959cc V6 twin-cam
Power:	220hp @ 6300rpm
Torque:	270Nm (199lb ft) @ 5000rpm
Transmission:	6-speed manual
Wheels:	17in alloy
Weight:	1415kg
Top Speed:	154mph
0–62mph:	6.8sec

SPECIFICATIONS

SPIDER 2.0 JTS

Engine:	1970cc 4-cyl twin-cam
Power:	163hp @ 6400rpm
Torque:	206Nm (152lb ft) @ 3250rpm
Transmission:	5-speed manual
Wheels:	17in alloy
Weight:	1405kg
Top speed:	140mph
0–62mph:	8.4sec

The GTV was facelifted in 2003, featuring a different front end treatment.

Expanded 3.2-litre engine was the ultimate development of the Busso V6.

The deeper Alfa 147-inspired front grille is clear in this shot of a Phase III Spider.

From the rear, the facelifted "Phase III" Spider looked hardly any different from before.

From the front, the GT looked like an Alfa 147 hatchback but it had its own unique style.

Giugiaro designed the clever GT, which was based on an Alfa 156 estate platform.

GT (2003-2010)

The GT was a curious mongrel of a car in many ways, but ultimately a sum far greater than its parts. Although the GT was a new model in Alfa's line-up, it was a mash-up of existing models, being based on the floorpan of the 156 Sportwagon, with the bulkhead and dashboard taken from the 147. On paper, this may have seemed a little disappointing – both these models were already getting long in the tooth by this stage – but it was a good way to keep costs down and speed up the development process. The GT's sporting pretensions were enhanced by the floorpan receiving some beefing up, adding a claimed 15 per cent to the torsional rigidity. It used double wishbone front suspension and a multi-link rear set-up using struts and coil springs.

The GT's shape was designed by Bertone, and was widely praised: compact, sleek and low-slung, with a

SPECIFICATIONS	
GT 3.2 V6	
Engine:	3179cc V6 twin-cam
Power:	240hp @ 6200rpm
Torque:	289Nm (213lb ft) @ 4800rpm
Transmission:	6-speed manual
Wheels:	17in alloy
Weight:	1410kg
0-62mph:	6.7 sec
Top speed:	151mph

This was a highly practical coupé, with seating for five and a tailgate opening up to a big boot.

sharply contoured and well-proportioned rear half. This was a much more practical proposition than the Tipo 916 GTV, being a full five-seater with a sizeable boot accessed by a hatchback, plus folding rear seats.

First seen at the 2003 Geneva Motor Show, it actually took 10 months before the GT went on sale. At launch, it was available with a 2.0-litre JTS direct-injection four-cylinder petrol engine (165hp) and a 1.9-litre JTD turbodiesel (150hp, later 170hp). After a few months, a 240hp 3.2-litre V6 joined the range, borrowing its Busso V6 from the GTV – making the GT the very last car to use the Busso V6. In this form, Alfa claimed a top speed of 151mph and a 0–62mph time of 6.7 seconds. A 1.8-litre petrol unit also became available in time. Manual transmission was most common, with the option of Selespeed semi-automatic being less favoured by owners. The GT was greeted as a fine-handling yet comfortable and practical coupé.

The GT lasted in production far longer than most people expected. It straddled the GTV and Brera eras, running side-by-side with the GTV until the latter's demise in 2006. The GT should have been overshadowed by the Alfa 159-based Brera launched in 2005, but in fact the two models were sold in Alfa dealerships until 2010, with the GT performing so well that Alfa felt it couldn't axe it before then. A grand total of 80,832 GTs had been made by the end of the line – far more than the contemporary 916 GTV and Brera, in fact.

Heresy? Alfa offered diesel power in the GT – a first for a sporting Alfa.

The GT's dashboard was essentially shared with the Alfa 147.

The production Brera shared much with the original concept car and was widely praised in design circles.

Giorgetto Giugiaro stands in front of his 2002 Brera concept car.

BRERA & SPIDER (2005-2010)

Alfa Romeo's Brera coupé was born, in concept form at least, at the 2002 Geneva Motor Show, where the Italdesign stand displayed a 2+2 show proposal. Although badged an Alfa Romeo, it was in fact based on the mechanicals of the Maserati 4200 coupé.

Alfa management was impressed enough by Italdesign's concept that it was persuaded to go ahead with a production version. It would be a further three years before the showroom-ready Brera finally arrived in 2005, and when it did, it looked remarkably close to the original, although it swapped the concept car's scissor doors for conventional ones. Another big difference was the mechanical basis: Maserati was gone, and the platform of the Alfa Romeo 159 was substituted, complete with double wishbone front and multi-link rear suspension. Initially, this platform had been conceived as the basis of a new Saab model, and since Alfa Romeo was by now cooperating with General Motors (Saab's owner), it was given access to it.

As a stylish 2+2 coupé, the Brera was the natural successor to the 916 GTV, although it was somewhat less practical than the five-seater Alfa Romeo GT that had recently been introduced. The front bodywork was essentially the same as the 159's, complete with its dramatic six-lamp nose, but aft of that was an all-new coupé shape that was widely appreciated, even if the front and rear overhangs were somewhat oversized, giving the proportions an odd look when viewed from the side. The 159-based cabin was plush enough, although the rear seats were pretty cramped. The boot was accessed via a rear hatch and was, at 300 litres, fair-sized by coupé standards, if not as big as the GT's.

Despite the idea for the car being Italdesign's (as

well as the body design), Giugiaro's company received something of a slap in the face when it was Pininfarina that was given the task of actually producing it.

Three engines were offered at launch: 185hp 2.2-litre four-cylinder JTS petrol, 200hp 2.4-litre five-cylinder diesel and 260hp 3.2-litre V6 (the latter – rather disappointingly for Alfa fans – derived from General Motors, rather than Alfa's own Busso unit, although Alfa did make its own changes to enhance performance). The first two models were only available with front-wheel drive, but the V6 came with Alfa's Q4 four-wheel drive system – the first production Alfa coupé ever to have 4x4. From 2008, a V6 model with Q2 two-wheel drive was also offered. From 2007, the diesel jumped in power to 210hp, while the 2009 model year saw new 2.0-litre 170hp diesel and a 1.75-litre 200hp petrol options. In addition to manual gearboxes, a Qtronic

While its front half was 159-based, the rear styling was unique, with a distinctive V-shaped rear window.

The Brera was offered with front-wheel drive or four-wheel drive, but in both cases proved rather heavy.

In the UK, rally specialist Prodrive was asked to develop the more focused, lighter Brera S.

Wraparound dashboard looked appealing but lack of space in the rear seats was criticised.

semi-automatic was also offered.

Since the Brera's considerable weight (1630kg in V6 form) blunted its performance and attracted criticisms from the press regarding its handling agility and braking, a version was specially developed for the UK market, in conjunction with the rally engineering company Prodrive. To create the so-called Prodrive S, the British company chose stiffer Eibach springs that lowered the ride height by 10mm, Bilstein dampers, uprated Brembo brakes and special 19-inch wheels. It insisted on front-wheel drive rather than four-wheel drive, which shed fully 100kg of weight in the 3.2 V6 model's case. The 2.2 JTS four-cylinder engine was also offered in Prodrive S guise, in this case the mods saving 35kg. Prodrive boss David Richards described the new model as "a great Italian product with an English flavour" and it came with a red, white and green Union Jack logo. Prodrive S versions were far better received by the press and are definitely favoured by buyers today thanks to their greater agility and sharper performance. One final twist in the Brera tale was that, towards the end of the its life (in 2009), a 1750 TBi model was added,

using Alfa's new 1742cc turbo engine with 200hp.

The open-top Brera-based Spider followed the coupé in 2006. This was jointly developed by Alfa Romeo and Pininfarina, and the latter's badges appeared on the body flanks. In one respect that was an unusual state of affairs, since the Giugiaro-designed Brera never had any such badging. Notable design touches included neat rollover hoops, aerodynamic head fairings and a soft-top that disappeared completely under a rear cover.

The Spider was offered with the same range of engines as the Brera: 2.2 JTS and 3.2 JTS V6 initially, plus a 2.4 JTDm diesel from 2007, and from 2009 new 1750 TBi and 2.0 JTDm diesel versions. Depending on the model, the Spider could be had with either front-wheel drive or all-wheel drive.

The Brera and Spider were frankly not the commercial successes that Alfa had hoped for. Over the Brera's five-year production life (2005 to 2010), a total of 21,786 were built, far fewer than the supposedly stop-gap GT model that sold alongside it. Alfa Romeo also made a further 12,488 Spiders from 2006 to 2010.

Controversially, the 3.2-litre V6 engine was not Alfa's Busso but based on a General Motors unit.

Without a roof, the Brera was transformed into the new Spider.

There was grip aplenty from the chassis, especially in 4x4 guise, but handling wasn't a Spider strong suit.

The UK launch for the Alfa Spider took place in Morocco.

Smart roll-over hoops distinguished the soft-top Spider.

S P E C I F I C A T I O N S	
BRERA V6	
Engine:	3195cc V6
Power:	260hp @ 6300rpm
Torque:	321Nm (237lb ft) @ 4500rpm
Transmission:	6-speed manual
Wheels:	18in alloy
Weight:	1630kg
Top Speed:	149mph
0–62mph:	6.8sec

S P E C I F I C A T I O N S	
SPIDER 2.2 JTS	
Engine:	2198cc four in-line
Power:	185hp @ 6500rpm
Torque:	230Nm (170lb ft) @ 4500rpm
Transmission:	6-speed manual
Wheels:	19in alloy
Weight:	1530kg
Top speed:	138mph
0–62mph:	8.8sec

The 8C Competizione was a very exotic, upmarket departure for Alfa Romeo.

Its styling was proudly the work of Alfa Romeo's own Centro Stile and a young Wolfgang Egger.

8C (2008-2009)

Giugiaro's Brera concept of 2002 not only gave birth to the Alfa Romeo Brera but also, in a roundabout way, the 8C Competizione. The original Brera concept was based on Maserati mechanicals, and since Maserati was now part of the Fiat/Alfa family, Alfa Romeo ran with the idea and produced an Alfa-badged sports car which inheritied much from its Modena-based sister marque.

The first 8C Competizione concept was shown at the 2003 Frankfurt Motor Show. When the production version finally arrived five years later, it looked remarkably similar. The sensational design was by Wolfgang Egger, who was then a fresh face at Alfa Romeo Centro Stile, and he said he drew inspiration from Alfa classics like the 1955 Sportiva, 1938 8C 2900 Le Mans and 1996 Nuvola concept.

The 8C used a shortened, rear-wheel drive Maserati coupé platform – very much the same configuration as Giugiaro's Brera prototype. Much of the structure and bodywork was carbonfibre, with a steel central floorpan and steel subframes front and rear. The engine was based on the then-new Maserati GranTurismo 4.7-litre V8 engine, and its output of 450hp at 7000rpm was very healthy. Although the car weighed a hefty 1585kg, it was certainly no slouch (with 284hp per tonne). Indeed, it had better performance than its bigger and heavier Maserati relative. Not only was acceleration excellent (0-62mph in 4.8 seconds) and the top speed 181mph – true supercar performance – the 8C also revelled in a superb symphony of noises from the engine and exhaust.

The double-wishbone suspension shared much in common with the Maserati Quattroporte V's but it

Potent 4.7-litre V8 engine was sourced from Maserati.

Few who drove the 8C were disappointed by its performance or handling ability.

It looked amazing, especially in special-order Rosso Competizione paint – a £20,000 option.

had unique bushes, geometry, springs and dampers – and no sign of Maserati's Skyhook damping. Despite the presence of a limited-slip differential, the rear end could skip out of line if provoked, but the handling was praised as being predictable and intuitive.

The author in his road test for *Auto Italia* magazine said: "The 8C has a brutality to its power, and yet also a relaxed feeling that there's plenty in reserve. The sound of the V8 is gorgeous, especially if you punch

the 'Sport' button which opens up the baffles in the exhaust, and also sharpens up the throttle response and prevents the auto 'box shifting up a gear when you hit the rev limiter."

The transmission was a robotised six-speed semi-automatic transaxle (the gearbox being sited just ahead of the rear axle) which was shared with the Ferrari F430. The driver could operate the 'box by paddle shifters, and it was capable of changing

Much of the 8C's structure was carbonfibre, with a steel centre section, steel subframes and Maserati-based suspension.

This was a true supercar, capable of 0-62mph in 4.8 seconds and a top speed of 181mph.

Wonderfully evocative cabin featured carbon and aluminium. Note the button-operated transmission.

cogs in 175 milliseconds, faster than anyone could move a manual gear lever, said Alfa. There were standard carbon ceramic brakes, while inside the car, carbon and aluminium adorned the two-seater cabin, including delightful carbon seats.

At launch in 2008, the 8C Competizione slotted in as a prestigious flagship, and was ideally timed to coincide with Alfa's brand relaunch in America. The 8C was even more expensive than Maserati's Gran Turismo, priced at over £130,000. Only ever built with its steering wheel on the left, a limited run of 500 8C coupés was constructed, all at the Maserati factory in Modena, 40 of which came to the UK officially.

A further run of 500 examples of a new convertible version, the 8C Spider, followed in 2009. The Spider featured carbon strengthening to address lost rigidity and a two-layer electrically folding soft-top, plus softer suspension settings than the coupé, while adding some 90kg to overall weight.

Like the coupé, only 500 examples of the 8C Spider were ever made.

Spider featured an elegant fabric roof that folded electronically, but added 90kg in weight.

S P E C I F I C A T I O N S

8C

Engine:	4691cc V8
Power:	450hp @ 7000rpm
Torque:	491Nm (362lb ft) @ 4750rpm
Transmission:	6-speed sequential
Wheels:	20in alloy
Weight:	1585kg (Spider: 1675kg)
Top Speed:	181mph
0-62mph:	4.8sec

4C (2013-)

With the mid-engined 4C coupé of 2013, Alfa Romeo once again broke new ground.

The radical, and in many ways unique, 4C actually began life as an Abarth project. Alfa Romeo was all set to have a new Spider sharing the architecture of the fourth-generation Mazda MX-5, but FCA management decided to swap the projects around, giving Fiat and Abarth what would become the 124 Spider, while it was Alfa Romeo that got the ex-Abarth 4C.

The decision was probably wise. In the 4C was a highly advanced mid-engined sports car that better suited Alfa's brand character. The chassis was perhaps the most radical aspect of all. Developed by the racing car company Dallara, it was a carbonfibre tub weighing just 65kg. Aluminium was used to reinforce the roof and the front and rear beams. Composite SMC (Sheet Moulding Compound) was used for the bodywork, shaving 20% off weight compared to a steel shell. Another curious design feature was the "spider's eye" headlamps consisting of multiple small bulbs.

Although the 4C's mid-mounted 1742cc four-cylinder engine shared similarities with the Giulietta unit of the same capacity, it actually marked a significant evolution. Delivering its 240hp power with the character of a much larger engine, the turbo was tuned to offer 80% of peak torque at just 1800rpm, meaning gear changes were not often required. There was never a manual transmission option for the 4C, only a "TCT" six-speed dual-dry-clutch automated/paddle-shift system, complete with a launch control function.

The 4C had Alfa's DNA system, featuring

Dynamic, Natural and All Weather driving modes, plus a Race setting which left the electronic Q2 differential switched on, but deactivated the stability control and ABS systems, while a neat g-meter came up on the dashboard and the exhaust became much louder. A popular extra was the Racing Pack consisting of extra carbonfibre for the interior, revised springs and dampers, thicker anti-roll bars, a sports exhaust and larger wheels. The brakes – perforated, ventilated, 305x28 discs, grabbed by Brembo four-pot callipers – went about their work with great efficacy.

With a weight of just 925kg, the 4C was very rapid indeed. Road testers enthused about almost every aspect of how it drove, but the 4C did acquire a reputation in some circles for nervousness, since the steering and suspension geometry were set up more for track use, and some drivers felt it was too twitchy on real world roads. As Richard Bremner put it in *Auto Italia* magazine: "This car darts, weaves and redirects itself like a puppy chasing scents."

The public first saw the 4C in concept form at the March 2011 Geneva Show, but it would be two years before the production car arrived, with the first buyers waiting until 2014 for delivery. The price of around £45,000 put it firmly in Porsche territory, but no other car had the 4C's unique combination of facets. Annual production of 3500 units was mooted at Maserati's Modena plant, but this figure was never reached. Around 1000 units per year were sold in Europe, and a further 500-600 per year in the USA.

In 2016, when the 4C Spider arrived (see below), the coupé was given extra standard equipment such

Ultra-rigid carbon tub enabled super-sharp handling.

Extremely light – weighing just 925kg – the 4C was very fast despite its relatively modest 240hp.

as bi-LED headlamps with carbonfibre surrounds, raising the price to £51,500. Production of the 4C coupé ended in 2018, but this was not the only 4C model to be built. 2014 had seen the debut of the targa-roof 4C Spider, with a fabric top that could be removed, rolled up and stowed in the boot. Gone was the coupé's sloping fastback, replaced by a new roll-over structure, flying buttresses and a curved engine lid, which had the effect of improving rear visibility. Rigidity was not really affected, so it drove much the same as the coupé. The roof and extra strengthening added 15.5kg to the car's weight, and the Spider ended up being 45kg heavier because of its extra standard equipment, including air conditioning, parking sensors and leather dashboard, plus less controversial faired-in xenon headlamps. It also added £8000 to

the 4C's price. The 4C Spider remains on sale at the time of writing as the only two-door model in Alfa Romeo's range.

SPECIFICATIONS

4C

Engine:	1742cc 4-cyl turbo
Max power:	240hp at 6000rpm
Max torque:	350Nm (258lb ft) at 2100-4000rpm
Transmission:	6-speed dual-clutch semi-auto
Wheels:	17 or 18in front, 18 or 19in rear, alloy
Weight:	895kg (Spider: 940kg)
0-62mph:	4.5sec
Top speed:	155mph

Targa-roof 4C Spider featured more conventional headlamps than the coupé.

The fabric roof rolled up and was stowed in the front luggage compartment.

Exposed carbon, digital dashboard and paddle-shift gear change featured in a very focused cabin.

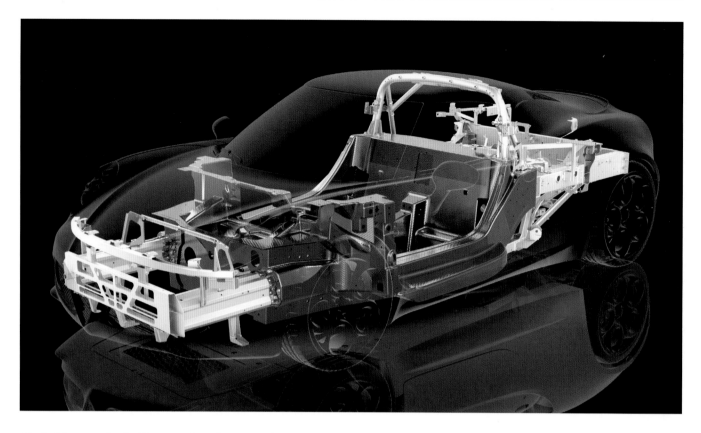

Metal subframe joined carbonfibre main tub in what was a revolutionary chassis.

Mid-mounted four-cylinder turbo engine was ideally placed for handling balance.

Alfa Romeo's Proteo of 1991 prepared the public for the forthcoming GTV/Spider.

Proteo was Alfa 164-based and featured four-wheel drive and four-wheel steering.

Nuvola of 1996 had a separate chassis, aiming to revive coachbuilding traditions.

Wonderful shape was the responsibility of Alfa Romeo's Walter de Silva.

Curious Alfa Romeo Centauri concept of 1999 was a student proposal.

ALFAS THAT MIGHT HAVE BEEN

Although it would not be unveiled until 1994, the shape of the 916 GTV had already been set in 1988. To prepare the public for the radical shape of this newcomer, Alfa Romeo presented the Proteo in 1991, which featured the same rising belt-line and bonnet headlamp cut-outs that would make the GTV/Spider so distinctive. Unlike the GTV/Spider, the Proteo was based on the Alfa 164 and featured four-wheel drive (making it the first ever 4x4 Alfa coupé), four-wheel steering and removable glass roof panels.

Another very striking Alfa Romeo concept car was the Nuvola, shown at the 1996 Paris Salon. Alfa's design boss, Walter de Silva, was responsible for its shape, and he and his team drew inspiration from Alfa's glory days of the past, not only in the Nuvola's proportion and detailing but in one important aspect of its construction, too. The Nuvola had a separate chassis, in theory allowing any body shape to be designed around it – which would, effectively, have revived a long-lost coachbuilding tradition, had the Nuvola gone into production. De Silva's design was extremely elegant: a long, classic bonnet; low, tapering rear; recessed lights and lots of chrome. Despite the retro flavour, it was also ultra-modern: 300hp aluminium V6 engine, four-wheel drive and six speeds. For a while, it seemed like the Nuvola would become a production model, but sadly that never happened.

One final "official" Alfa project came about in 1999, when a group of young designers working at the Fiat Department for Design Development and Car Innovation, near Milan, came up with the Alfa Centauri concept. This was never a production prospect, more of a simple design exercise, and was notable for its short front and rear overhangs, crisp lines and the ability to have its steering wheel switched from left to right very easily. The chassis was made of aluminium, the engine was Alfa's 3.0-litre V6 and the drive was to all four wheels.

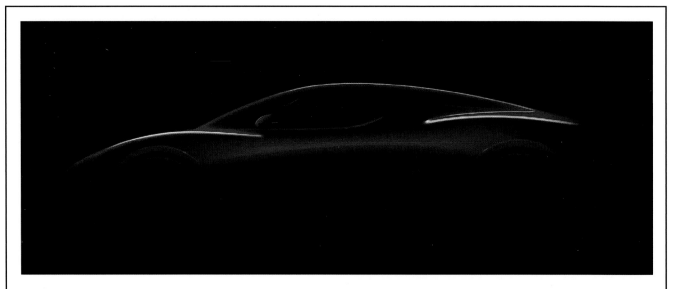

The new-for-2022 Alfa Romeo 8C is set to be a mid-engined supercar.

Alfa Romeo promised buyers a GTV, a two-door coupé version of the Giulia saloon.

FUTURE ALFA COUPÉS

In June 2018, Alfa Romeo's future was laid out by the CEO of Fiat Chrysler Automobiles, Sergio Marchionne, in a five-year plan that was delivered one month before his tragic death. He revealed that two exciting new sports coupé models would be launched by 2022. The first was a new 8C coupé, the natural successor to the 2007-2010 8C Competizione. Unlike its predecessor, though, it would be mid-engined and a hybrid, capable of developing more than 700hp courtesy of "E-Boost" electrically-assisted turbocharging and a pair of electric motors at the front end (in turn giving it four-wheel drive capability). Alfa quoted a sub-3.0 second 0-62mph time. In the teaser image released by Alfa, you could see clear design inspiration from the 1967 33 Stradale. Alfa also said the new 8C would be built around a carbonfibre monocoque.

The other new coupé model was set to revive the defunct GTV badge, and was essentially a two-door coupé version of the existing Giulia, built on Alfa's "Giorgio" platform. This was billed as a four-seater coupé with perfect 50/50 weight distribution. Alfa said the Giulia Quadrifoglio's 2.9-litre V6 engine would have its power boosted to over 640hp thanks to electric "E-Boost" turbocharging, while more affordable 2.0-litre engines from the Giulia saloon also would join the range.